In the Spirit
of Saint Alphonsus

Thirty Prayer Services
for the Church Year

With Six in Spanish

Terrence J. Moran, C.Ss.R.

Translated by Ruskin Piedra, C.Ss.R., and Lucía Pérez
Illustrated by Sister Trinita Marie Amorosi, I.H.M.

Liguori

LIGUORI, MISSOURI

Special thanks is due to the staff of Liguori Publications for their interest in this manuscript from the beginning: Father Harry Grile, C.Ss.R., Brother Daniel Korn, C.Ss.R., and members of the Mission Sponsorship Team: Judy Bauer, editor; Israel Martinez, Libros Liguori editorial assistant; Cecelia Portlock, production editor; Pam Hummelsheim, art director; and Grady Gunter, cover designer. A debt of gratitude is owed as well to those Redemptorists who are models to me of commitment to the spirit of Saint Alphonsus: my novice masters, Father Carl Hoegerl, C.Ss.R., and Father Walter Karrer, C.Ss.R., Father Matthew Allman, C.Ss.R., Father J. Robert Fenili, C.Ss.R., and Daniel Francis, C.Ss.R.

Published by Liguori Publications
Liguori, Missouri
http://www.liguori.org
http://www.catholicbooksonline.com

Library of Congress Cataloging-in-Publication Data

Moran, Terrence, C.Ss.R.
     In the spirit of Saint Alphonsus : thirty prayer services for the church year : with six in Spanish / Terrence J. Moran ; [illustrated by] Trinita Marie Amorosi.—1st. ed.
          p.   cm.
     ISBN 0-7648-0667-X (pbk.)
     1. Redemptorists—Liturgy—Texts. I. Title.

BX2049.R4 A1   2000
267'.0272—dc21   00–042827

CONTENTS

Part Three: Prayer on Redemptorist Themes

INTRODUCTION

> *God does not disdain, but rather delights, that you speak with that confidence, that freedom and tenderness, which children use toward their mothers. Hear how God invites us to come to his lap and the caresses he promises to bestow on us: As nurslings, you shall be carried in her arms and fondled in her lap; As a mother comforts her sons, so will I comfort you (Isa 66:12). As a mother delights to place her little children upon her knees and so to feed or to caress them, with like tenderness does our gracious God delight to treat those beloved souls who have given themselves totally to God and placed in God's goodness all their confidence.*

These lovely words of Saint Alphonsus Liguori are found at the beginning of his work *The Way to Converse With God*. They express the vision of God that motivated his long life of apostolic ministry. Freedom and tenderness were what Alphonsus worked to convey to a world for whom God was a Jansenist tyrant or a remote Prime Mover. It is unquestionable that prayer, individual and communal, is a central value of Redemptorist life and spirituality. Saint Alphonsus Liguori is often called the "Doctor of Prayer," and he said that no matter what the theme of his sermons seemed to be the real topic was always prayer. Of the various constitutive elements of Redemptorist community outlined in Chapter Three of our Constitutions and Statutes, prayer is given the first place. The Constitutions set high standards for Redemptorist prayer. We are to make every effort to have Saint Alphonsus's spirit of prayer in our own lives (Chapter 2, Article 3, Paragraph 26). Each community is obliged to discover new forms of community prayer which will give expression to the unity of the members and foster our missionary zeal (Chapter 2, Article 3, Paragraph 30).

A number of factors have contributed to a renewed interest among Redemptorists in the spiritual patrimony of the Congregation: the celebrations of the Tercentenary of the Birth of Saint Alphonsus (1696–1996); and the emphasis placed by the last two General Chapters of Redemptorist spirituality (1991, 1997); the flourishing of research into

Alphonsian spirituality in the years since the Second Vatican Council. In many parts of the Congregation, laypeople, and especially young people, are looking for a more intimate share in Redemptorist spirituality by joining with us in prayer and apostolic ministry.

The Twenty-First General Chapter held in Itaici, Brazil, called the Congregation "to make an effort to find new forms which shape our spirituality, in accord with the social and ecclesial reality of each unit" (Final Document, 34, c) and "to search out, in conformity with our tradition and style of life, simple forms and familiar ways in which we can pray and teach others to pray" (Final Document, 41, c). *In the Spirit of Saint Alphonsus: Thirty Prayer Services for the Church Year* is intended to be a contribution to fulfilling that goal of the General Chapter.

Since the Second Vatican Council, communal celebration of the Liturgy of the Hours has become the most typical form of common prayer in the entire Congregation. This is a development called for by the Constitutions themselves (General Statute 028b) and recaptures Alphonsus's own love for the Liturgy of the Hours. Many confreres have felt the need to complement the Liturgy of the Hours with forms of prayer that are more personal and that draw more explicitly on the Congregation's own heritage of prayer. The prayer tradition of the Congregation was rich in symbol and gesture, sound and silence. Our traditional prayer forms relied heavily on silent meditation in common. The language of our community prayer was often poetically rich and emotionally evocative. Our prayer tradition also used movement and gesture effectively: bowing and prostration, extending the arms, processions.

The prayer services in this collection attempt to offer a resource for community prayer that both draws on our Redemptorist tradition and which accords with the realities of Redemptorist life at the dawn of the third millennium. *In the Spirit of Alphonsus* offers thirty prayer services divided into three sections.

PART ONE: PRAYING WITH ALPHONSUS THROUGH THE CHURCH YEAR

These services draw on the works of Saint Alphonsus and symbols from the Redemptorist tradition as a way of prayerfully celebrating the seasons of the liturgical year: Advent, Christmas, Lent, Easter, Pentecost, and Ordinary Time. While they draw on Redemptorist sources, they are not intended for use by Redemptorists alone. They can be suitably used for times of prayer and reflection with parish groups, staffs, prayer groups, lay associates. They attempt to make the riches of Alphonsian spirituality available to a wider audience.

PART TWO: PRAYING THE REDEMPTORIST FEASTS

These services are intended for Redemptorist community prayer on celebrations of special people and events in the Congregation's history. There are services for our titular feast of the Most Holy Redeemer and for the anniversary of our foundation; for our two special Marian celebrations, Immaculate Conception and Our Lady of Perpetual Help; celebrations of our special patrons Joseph and Teresa of Ávila; celebrations of our canonized and beatified confreres; celebrations of other holy people in our history such as the Venerable Maria Celeste Crostarosa, and especially those in North America such as Blessed Francis X. Seelos and Alfred Pampalon. While these services presume that the people praying them are Redemptorists, they can be easily adapted to include others.

PART THREE: PRAYER ON REDEMPTORIST THEMES

These services are centered on a variety of themes. Some are solidly traditional, celebrating the central themes of Alphonsian spirituality and our tradition of Marian devotion. Some focus on riches of our heritage to which we seldom avert: our tradition of spiritual direction; the pioneer experience of the Congregation in the United States; our Constitutions and Statutes as a source of Redemptorist spirituality. Some attempt to bring an Alphonsian perspective on contemporary concerns and to uncover neglected aspects of our tradition: Alphonsian spirituality and ecology, the laity, and the feminine.

Each of the prayer services tries to integrate the following elements:

1. SCRIPTURE

Our Constitutions tell us that since we are called to preach the Word of God we must be abundantly nourished by it (Chapter 4, Article 3, Paragraph 81). An attempt has been made to make the Word of God central to each service. This is done in various ways—by biblical readings, using the words of psalms and other scripture as prayer, by use of biblical motifs and imagery. As Saint Alphonsus reminds us, nothing is better able to enkindle the love of God in us than the Word of God itself.

2. REDEMPTORIST TRADITION

The services draw explicitly on the lives and writings of our holy confreres as resources for prayer. Preeminent among these are the example and writings of Saint Alphonsus. Our Constitutions (Chapter 2, Article 3, Paragraph 33) tell us we must have very much at heart the development in our own lives of Alphonsus's way of thinking with the Church since this is a sound criterion of our missionary service. The services frequently use the writings of Alphonsus and our other sainted confreres for readings and prayers. While remaining faithful to their thought, some editing and revision of language has been done to make these writings a contemporary source for prayer.

3. FAITH-SHARING

In nearly all the services, opportunity is provided for a period of faith-sharing, and some suggested questions are offered as "thought starters." The Final Document of the Twenty-First General Chapter says that Redemptorist community should be identifiable by "a sense in our daily life that it is God who calls us and it is the Spirit of Christ who unites us and leads us on to an ever deeper community" (27). This is hardly possible unless we take the time to share with one another our experience of the movement of God's Spirit in our lives and listen receptively to our confreres as they do the same. Each community is free to adapt this faith-sharing to its own particular circumstances. While the prayer services suggest that this faith-sharing is optional, the prayer experience will be more rich if some faith-sharing is attempted. The rewards that come from our efforts to share with one another on a deeper level more than compensate for the awkwardness we may experience in the attempt.

4. SYMBOL AND RITUAL

Nearly all the services include some ritual or symbolic gesture that relates to the theme of the service. Some are drawn from Redemptorist tradition; others break open the meaning of Redemptorist symbols in new ways. Each service also contains suggestions for the environment of the prayer space. Redemptorist tradition from the earliest days showed a great sensitivity to beauty and an effective use of ceremony and gesture. These services try to recapture and revive that tradition. The person who prepares the prayer should be careful that the ritual gestures are well integrated into the flow of the prayer and are not overburdened with verbal explanations. A symbol which needs extensive explanation is rarely effective.

5. MUSIC

Saint Alphonsus is unique among the canonized saints for the variety and popularity of his musical compositions. Redemptorist missions employed music skillfully, and Redemptorist churches from Saint Benno's onward were renowned for the splendor of their liturgical music. It speaks volumes about the Redemptorist commitment to music that the pioneers of the American mission wandered the American frontier with a portable organ among their baggage. The services include suggestions for sung or instrumental music. All the suggestions can be found in four sources:

- *Gather Comprehensive* (Chicago: GIA Publications, 1994)
- *Glory and Praise* (Phoenix, AZ: North American Liturgy Resources, 1987)
- *Worship* (Chicago: GIA Publications, 1986)
- *S. Alfonso de Liguori: Les chants populaires en version instrumentale*, available from Musique pour le monde; 11, Vézina; L'Ange Gardien; Quebec, Canada G0A 2K0. It is unfortunate that the music of Saint Alphonsus, the most accomplished musicians among the canonized saints, is not better known. Several of the services recommend use of Alphonsus's music which may be found on a compact disk commissioned by the Sainte Anne de Beaupré Province.
- The Spanish songs are taken from *Flor y Canto*, Oregon Catholic Press, 1989.

To avoid copyright difficulties, the songs were not reproduced. The suggestions were given with an eye to fittingness and familiarity. Those who use these prayer services are certainly free to make other choices, but prayer without song could hardly be faithful to the Alphonsian tradition.

6. SILENCE

Meditation made in common was the characteristic Redemptorist prayer for most of our history, and it remains a cherished practice in many of our communities. Silence and solitude were the most essential elements of a retreat according to Saint Alphonsus; to enter into the desert where God speaks to the heart. Although liturgical norms for both the Eucharist and the Liturgy of the Hours provide for the integration of periods of silence, these are most often ignored. Most of the prayer services call for pauses for silent prayer and some for extended periods. The richness of the language of our tradition requires periods of silent reflection for personal integration; and the prayer leader should be sensitive to this.

7. CONTEMPORARY RELEVANCE

Saint Alphonsus was so steeped in the language and concerns of his age that many people, and even confreres, today find it difficult to relate to him. Every attempt has been made to use language that is as contemporary and inclusive as possible. Sometimes respect for a text from another generation makes use of completely inclusive language impossible. Some of the services reflect concerns that would have been alien to Alphonsus but certainly would not be foreign to his expansive zeal were he alive today.

8. FLEXIBILITY

These prayer services are intended to be a resource. To be effective they require adaptation to the interests and concerns of the local community at prayer. It would be a mistake in many circumstances simply to run off copies of these services for communal use. The more a praying community makes these services their own, the greater their potential as effective instruments for prayer.

9. ART

Redemptorists owe a special debt of gratitude for the beautiful original artwork that graces this book. Sister Trinita Marie Amorosi is a Sister, Servant of the Immaculate Heart of Mary of Immaculata, Pennsylvania, and a professor of art at Immaculata College. The IHMs were founded by a Redemptorist, Louis Florent Gillet, and Mother Teresa Maxis, a great lover of Saint Alphonsus. They share our spirituality and are proud to be considered members of the Alphonsian family. Therefore Sister Trinita brings to her work a special sensitivity for the Redemptorist spiritual tradition. Most of the prayer services are illustrated by one of her works. Besides adding beauty to the work, they also serve to provide us with a body of "Redemptorist clip art" that can be used in other circumstances. May the God of Loveliness richly bless Sister Trinita for her generous sharing of her gifts with us.

The purpose of this collection of prayer services would not be fulfilled if it only served to make the Redemptorist spiritual tradition a little better known and a little more loved. Our goal is that of Saint Alphonsus Liguori himself—to make us, his brothers and sisters grow in love of Jesus Christ and in commitment to his mission. With Alphonsus and our confreres throughout history we repeat the words of the Redeemer that have always had a special echo in the Redemptorist heart:

> The Spirit of the Lord has swept over us.
> Waves of the oil of election have been lavished over us:
> to announce amazing plenty to the poor;
> to set the doors of prisons swinging open;
> to dazzle darkened eyes with light;
> to lead shackled legs to dance in freedom;
> to proclaim that our time and place,
> all time and every place,
> can rest in the gaze of God's delight.

FREEDOM and TENDERNESS

CSSR

PART ONE

PRAYING WITH ALPHONSUS DURING THE CHURCH YEAR

PRAYING WITH ALPHONSUS DURING ADVENT

Environment: In a prominent location are placed nine candles. Prior to the beginning of the service, the presider asks nine participants to read and light a candle.

Opening Song

"O Come, O Come, Emmanuel": *Worship #357*
"Creator of the Stars of Night": *Worship #368*

Call to Prayer

Presider: Advent, when our northern hemisphere moves deeper into shadow, is a season, of darkness, of waiting for new birth. It is a time for us to reenter our own dark places as we wait once more for Emmanuel to be born within us. What may initially seem frightful, as her pregnancy must have surely seemed to Mary, can be transformed into a sacred place. The life of Alphonsus was full of Advent times. Often he had to wait in darkness for the birth of something new and unforeseen. We pray that he accompany us into our times of patient waiting and assist us by his example and prayers.

Pause for Silent Prayer

Reader 1: *Lights the first candle and says:* Alphonsus's friend and collaborator, Sister Maria Celeste Crostarosa, saw the pattern of our growth in Christian life as nine virtues. She chose the number nine because it is the number of the months a new life grows hidden in the darkness of the womb of its mother. She writes, "God speaks and says, 'Contemplate how truly you are like a little infant in the womb of its mother, living more its mother's life than its own. I am your Mother. I have given you birth in my womb by creation and, by my providence, I have protected you within the heart of my eternal love. I fed you and watched over you diligently. In everything be at rest: in troubles, in doubts, in fears, and temptations; in persecutions and humiliations bind yourself always to your dear mother's womb.' "

Pause for Silent Prayer

Reader 2: *Lights the second candle and says:* Alphonsus writes, "Behold the happy time is come which is called the fullness of time: When the fullness of time was come, God sent his Son…that he might redeem those who were crushed under the burden of the law."

Pause for Silent Prayer

Reader 3: *Lights the third candle and says:* Alphonsus writes, "The prophet Jeremiah foretold that God would create something new, a new child, to be the Redeemer: 'God has created a new thing upon the earth.' This new child is Jesus Christ."

Pause for Silent Prayer

Reader 4: *Lights the fourth candle and says:* Alphonsus writes, "Justly does the Apostle call Jesus Christ our life. Behold our Redeemer, clothed with flesh and become an Infant, and says to us, 'I have come that you might have life and have it to the full.'"

Pause for Silent Prayer

Reader 5: *Lights the fifth candle and says:* Alphonsus writes, "Your physician will come, says the prophet, to cure the sick; and he will come swiftly like the eagle, and like the sun, which on rising from the horizon, instantly sends its light to the other pole. But behold him, he is already come. Let us console ourselves and give thanks."

Pause for Silent Prayer

Reader 6: *Lights the sixth candle and says:* Alphonsus writes, "From the first moment of the Incarnation, Jesus embraced our redemption with enthusiasm. He rejoices like a giant to run his course and he comes leaping over the mountains and skipping over the hills."

Pause for Silent Prayer

Reader 7: *Lights the seventh candle and says:* Alphonsus writes, "The dawning light of God's coming startled the song bird awake and they broke the stillness of the long night. The chirping of the grasshopper gave voice to the joy of the silent earth."

Pause for Silent Prayer

Reader 8: *Lights the eighth candle and says:* Alphonsus writes, "The coming of our God soaks the earth like a summer shower and there blooms a hundred thousand fragrant flowers."

Reader 9: *Lights the ninth candle and says:* Alphonsus writes, "The coming of our God makes the fragrant vine to flower; its fruit hurries to ripen and the vine is heavy with grapes—Jesus himself is that luscious bundle of grapes whose fruit gives coolness to burning lips and whose drink gives warmth to the frozen heart."

Spontaneous Petitions

The lights in the room are extinguished and all pray in silence for a while. Then the presider invites all to prayer.

Presider: Let us now voice to God the needs hidden in the silence of our hearts. May our prayer give voice to the needs of the voiceless and bring into light the needs of those who live in shadows. We respond to each petition: "Come, oh come, Emmanuel."

Individuals offer spontaneous petitions and the assembly responds with "Come, oh come, Emmanuel" as indicated above.

The Our Father

Presider: With trust in God who nourishes and supports us, we now pray as Jesus taught us:

The assembly prays the Our Father.

Final Blessing

Presider: Please respond "Amen" to each part of this blessing that follows.
Presider: May God the Creator draw life out of our darkness.
All: Amen.
Presider: May Jesus Emmanuel be our companion.
All: Amen.
Presider: May the Holy Spirit fill us with longing for God's reign.
All: Amen.

Praying
with
Alphonsus
during
ADVENT

REZANDO CON ALFONSO EN ADVIENTO

Ambiente: En un lugar apropiado se colocan nueve velas.

Canto de entrada

"Oh Ven, Oh Ven, Emmanuel": *Flor y Canto #1*

Llamada a la Oración

Guía: El adviento, la estación en la cual nuestro hemisferio entra más y más profundamente en la sombra, es estación de quietud, de obscuridad, de esperanza de nuevo nacimiento. Es tiempo para nosotros de entrar en nuestros propios lugares obscuros mientras esperamos una vez más que nazca Emmanuel en nosotros. Lo que al principio nos parece ser motivo de temor, como seguramente habrá aparecido su embarazo a María, se puede transformar en lugar sagrado. La vida de Alfonso estuvo llena de tiempos de adviento. Muchas veces tuvo que esperar Alfonso en la obscuridad para el nacimiento de algo nuevo e imprevisto. Rezamos que él nos acompañe en los tiempos de paciente espera y que nos asista con su ejemplo y sus oraciones.

Una pausa para orar en silencio

Lector/a 1: *(encienda la primera vela y diga):* La amiga y colaboradora de Alfonso, Sor María Celeste Crostarosa, vió el modelo de nuestro crecimiento en la vida cristiana en forma de nueve virtudes. Ella escogió el número nueve por ser el número de meses en que una vida nueva crece escondida en la obscuridad del vientre materno. Ella escribe: "Dios habla y dice, 'Contempla lo mucho que te asemejas a un bebé en el vientre de su madre, viviendo más la vida de la madre que la suya. Yo soy tu Madre. Yo te he dado a luz en mi vientre por la creación, y por mi providencia, te he protegido dentro del corazón de mi amor eterno. Te alimenté y te guardé con esmero. En todo estate tranquilo: en los problemas, en las dudas, en los temores y en las tentaciones; en las persecuciones y en las humillaciones quédate atado siempre al vientre de tu querida madre.'"

Lector/a 2: *(encienda la segunda vela y diga):* Escribe Alfonso, "Mira que ha llegado el momento feliz que se llama la plenitud de los tiempos: Cuando llegó la plenitud de los tiempos, Dios envió a su Hijo…para rescatar a los que estaban agobiados bajo la carga de la ley."

Una pausa para orar en silencio

Lector/a 3: *(encienda la tercera vela y diga):* Escribe Alfonso: "El profeta Jeremías predijo que Dios crearía algo nuevo, un nuevo niño, que sería el Redentor: 'Dios ha creado algo nuevo sobre la tierra.' Este nuevo niño es Jesucristo."

Una pausa para orar en silencio

Lector/a 4: *(encienda la cuarta vela y diga):* Escribe Alfonso, "Justamente llama el Apóstol a Jesucristo nuestra vida. He aquí al Redentor, vestido de carne y hecho un niño, y nos dice, 'Yo he venido para que tengan vida y la tengan en abundancia.'"

Una pausa para orar en silencio

Lector/a 5: *(encienda la quinta vela y diga):* Escribe Alfonso, "Vendrá tu médico, dice el profeta, a curar a los enfermos; vendrá rápidamente como el águila, y como el sol, que cuando se eleva del horizonte, enseguida envía su luz al otro polo. Pero míralo, ya ha llegado. Consolémosnos y demos gracias."

Una pausa para orar en silencio

Lector/a 6: *(encienda la sexta vela y diga):* Escribe Alfonso, "Desde el primer momento de la Encarnación, Jesús abrazó nuestra redención con entusiasmo. Se regocija como gigante a correr su carrera y viene saltando por las montañas y brincando por las colinas."

Una pausa para orar en silencio

Lector/a 7: *(encienda la séptima vela y diga):* Escribe Alfonso, "La luz del amanecer de la llegada de Dios asustó al pájaro cantor y despertó y rompieron la tranquilidad de la larga noche. El chirrear del saltamontes dió voces al gozo de la tierra silenciosa."

Una pausa para orar en silencio

Lector/a 8: *(encienda la octava vela y diga):* La llegada de nuestro Dios empapa la tierra como lluvia veraniega y brotan cien mil flores fragantes.

Una pausa para orar en silencio

Lector/a 9: *(encienda la novena vela y diga):* Escribe Alfonso, "La venida de nuestro Dios hace que la viña fragante florezca; su fruta se apura en madurar y la viña está cargada de uvas, Jesús mismo es ese suculento racimo de uvas cuya fruta da frescura a los labios ardientes y cuyo trago da calor al corazón congelado."

Peticiones espontáneas

Se a pagan las luces en el cuarto y todos rezan en silencio por un tiempo. Luego el presidente invita a todos a rezar.

Guía: Elevemos ahora nuestras voces a Dios por las necesidades escondidas en el silencio de nuestros corazones. Que nuestra oración dé voces a las necesidades de los que no tienen voz y traiga a la luz las necesidades de aquellos que viven en sombras. Respondemos a cada petición: Ven, o ven, Emmanuel.

Padre Nuestro

Guía: Con confianza en Dios quien nos alimenta y sostiene, oremos como Jesús nos enseño:

La asamblea reza el Padre Nuestro.

Bendición final

Guía: Favor de responder "Amén" a cada parte de esta bendición:

— Que Dios el Creador saque vida de nuestras tinieblas.
— Que Jesús Emmanuel sea nuestro compañero.
— Que el Espíritu Santo nos llene de anhelos por el reino de Dios.

Rezando con Alfonso en ADVIENTO

2

PRAYING WITH ALPHONSUS AT CHRISTMAS

Environment: Prominently display a manger scene and a copy of the Bible opened to the Infancy Narrative of Luke, surrounded by a number of candles.

Opening Song

Any suitable Christmas carol may be used to open this prayer service.

Introduction

Presider: I bring you good news of great joy.
All: For this day is born for us a Savior.

First Reading

As the candles are lighted around the crib scene, the following words of Alphonsus are read:

Reader 1: The Jews kept a solemn festival called by them "the day of fire" in memory of the fire with which the prophet Nehemiah consumed the sacrifice upon their return from captivity in Babylon. (See 2 Maccabees 1:18–23.) With more reason should we call Christmas day the day of fire. On this day God came as a little child to cast the fire of love into the hearts of humanity.

The reader holds aloft the Bible while all greet the word of God, singing the following refrain. (See Worship #376.)

All: *Gloria in excelsis Deo, Gloria in excelsis Deo.* The assembly sings this refrain from "Angels We Have Heard on High."

Second Reading

Reader 2: Luke 2:1–15 (the Infancy Narrative).
All: The assembly sings the refrain.

Response

Presider: The following response is from the writings of Alphonsus on the Incarnation.
All: For us…
Presider: the Eternal Word became human.
All: For us…
Presider: the Eternal Word being great becomes little.
All: For us…
Presider: the Eternal Word from being a lord becomes a servant.
All: For us…
Presider: the Eternal Word being innocent takes on our guilt.
All: For us…
Presider: the Eternal Word being strong becomes weak.
All: For us…
Presider: the Eternal Word from being independent becomes dependent on us.
All: For us…
Presider: the Eternal Word from being happy shared our afflictions.
All: For us…
Presider: the Eternal Word from being rich became poor.
All: As above, the assembly sings *Gloria in Excelsis Deo. Gloria in Excelsis Deo.*

Third Reading

Reader 3: From the writings of Alphonsus on the Incarnation: "How happy the cave that witnesses the birth of the divine Word! How happy the manger that received the Lord of heaven! How happy the straw which served as a bed for the one who makes a throne upon the seraphim! Yes, happy that cave, that manger, that straw: happier still are those people who love such a Lord with fervor and tenderness. With what desire and pleasure does Jesus Christ enter into and rest in a heart that loves him!"

Presider: As we listen to the famous Christmas carol of Saint Alphonsus *"Tu scendi dalle stelle"* let us become aware of the Word-made-flesh present in our flesh.

The assembly listens in silence to an instrumental recording of "Tu scendi dalle stelle."

Faith-Sharing

Presider: The presider asks the following: By devotion to the Incarnation, Saint Alphonsus wanted us to see a God who shared human life not as an observer but as a participant. What emotions or experiences do we find it hard to imagine God sharing and why?

Each one present gives a response to the preceding question.

Intercessions

Presider: Alphonsus used to place a statue of the Infant Jesus at the head of the dining-room table, and his community would place food there to be given to the poor.

All: May our devotion to the Word-made-flesh make us more sensitive to the needs of our brothers and sisters.

Presider: Alphonsus wrote a lullaby that Mary would have sung to the child Jesus.

All: May our devotion to the Word-made-flesh enable us to calm the fears of the little and the weak and to give them rest.

Presider: As a bishop, Alphonsus opened a day-care center in his house for the children of peasant women who would come into town on market day.

All: May our devotion to the Word-made-flesh empower us to make our world a more just and welcoming place for the needs of women and children.

Presider: In his carol "*Tu scendi*," Alphonsus teaches us to look for God not in the starry perfection of the heavens but in our own world.

All: May our devotion to the Word-made-flesh gives us eyes to see the presence of God shining in and through the ordinary circumstances of human life.

Presider: In his meditations on the Incarnation, Alphonsus discovered and proclaimed a God who knew human need, poverty, and powerlessness.

All: May our devotion to the Word-made-flesh teach us to discover God in our experiences of need and loss of control.

The Our Father

Presider: With trust in God who nourishes and supports us, we now pray as Jesus taught:

The assembly prays the Our Father.

Sign of Peace

Presider: Alphonsus wrote, "Joy awoke at Jesus' birth and roamed creation free." In the joy of the Word-made-flesh let us offer to one another a sign of Christmas joy and peace.

Participants offer to one another a sign of peace.

Praying with Alphonsus at **CHRISTMAS**

REZANDO CON ALFONSO EN NAVIDAD

Ambiente: En un lugar apropiado despliegue una escena del pesebre y una copia de la biblia abierta en el relato de la infancia de Jesús en Lucas, rodeada de varias velas.

Canto de entrada

Cualquier villancico navideño apropiado.

Introdución

Guía: Les traigo una buena noticia de gran alegría.
Todos: Pues este día nos ha nacido un Salvador.

Primera Lectura

Mientras se encienden las velas alrededor del pesebre se leen las siguientes palabras de Alfonso:

Lector: Los judios mantenían un festival solemne llamado por ellos "el día de fuego" en memoria del fuego con que el profeta Nehemías consumió el sacrificio al retornar de la captividad en Babilonia. (Vea 2 Macabeos 1,18–23.) Con más razón debemos llamar al día de la Navidad el día de fuego. En este día Dios viene como un niñito para echar el fuego de amor en los corazones de la humanidad.

El lector eleva la biblia. Mientras todos a cantan el refrán del villancico navideño,

Todos: Gloria in excelsis Deo, Gloria in excelsis Deo.

Segunda Lectura

Lector: Lucas 2,1–15.

(todos cantan, "Gloria…, como arriba.")

Responsorio

(De los escritos de Alfonso sobre la Encarnación)

Todos: Por nosotros … (se repite antes de cada frase abajo)

Guía: …El verbo eterno se hizo hombre.

Todos: Por nosotros…

Guía:…El verbo eterno siendo grande se hizo pequeño.

Todos: Por nosotros…

Guía: …El verbo eterno de ser Señor se hizo siervo.

Todos: Por nosotros…

Guía:…El verbo eterno siendo inocente toma nuestra culpabilidad.

Todos: Por nosotros…

Guía: …El verbo eterno siendo fuerte se hace débil.

Todos: Por nosotros…

Guía: …El verbo eterno siendo independiente se hace depender de nosotros.

Todos: Por nosotros…

Guía: …El verbo eterno de ser feliz comparte nuestras preocupaciones.

Todos: Por nosotros…

Guía: …El verbo eterno de ser rico se hizo pobre.

Todos: (todos cantan, "Gloria…" como arriba.)

Tercera Lectura

Lector/a: De los escritos de Alfonso sobre la Encarnación: "¡Qué feliz la cueva que presenció el nacimiento del Verbo divino! ¡Qué feliz el pesebre que recibió al Señor de los cielos! ¡Qué feliz la paja que sirvió de cama para el que hace su trono sobre los querubines! Si, feliz esa cueva, ese pesebre, esa paja: más felices todavía aquellas personas que aman a tal Señor con fervor y ternura. ¡Con qué deseo y placer entra y descansa Jesucristo, en un corazón que le ama!"

Guía: Mientras escuchamos el famoso villancico navideño de San Alfonso *"Tu scendi dalle stelle,"* hagámonos conscientes del Verbo hecho carne presente en nuestra carne.

Todos escuchan en silencio la grabación instrumental de "Tu scendi dalle stelle."

Compartiendo la fe

Guía: Cada uno comparte con las personas cercanas o con todo el grupo su respuesta a la siguiente pregunta: Por su devoción a la Encarnación, San Alfonso quiso que nosotros viéramos a un Dios que comparte la vida humana, no como observador de afuera sino como participante.¿Qué emociones humanas o experiencias encontramos nosotros difíciles de imaginar que Dios comparte y por qué?

Cada uno de los presentes puede compartir su respuesta.

Peticiones

Guía: Alfonso solía colocar una estatua del Niño Jesús a la cabeza de la mesa del comedor y su comunidad solía poner allí comida para repartir a los pobres.

Todos: Que nuestra devoción al Verbo hecho carne nos haga más sensibles a las necesidades de nuestros hermanos y hermanas.

Guía: Alfonso escribió una canción de cuna que María hubiera cantado al Niño Jesús.

Todos: Que nuestra devoción al Verbo hecho carne nos ayude a calmar los temores de los pequeños y de los débiles y a darles descanso.

Guía: Como obispo Alfonso abrió un centro de cuidado en su casa para los niños de mujeres campesinas que venían al pueblo el día del mercado.

Todos: Que nuestra devoción al Verbo hecho carne nos habilite a hacer nuestro mundo un lugar más justo y acogedor para las necesidades de mujeres y niños.

Guía: En su villancico *"Tu scendi,"* Alfonso nos enseña a buscar a Dios no en la perfección estelar de los cielos, sino en nuestro propio mundo.

Todos: Que nuestra devoción al Verbo hecho carne nos dé ojos para ver la presencia de Dios brillando en y por las circunstancias ordinarias de la vida humana.

Guía: En su meditación sobre la Encarnación, Alfonso descubrió y proclamó a un Dios que conocía las necesidades humanas, la pobreza y la impotencia.

Todos: Que nuestra devoción al Verbo hecho carne nos enseñe a descubrir a Dios en nuestras experiencias de necesidad y pérdida de control.

Padre Nuestro

La asamblea reza el Padre Nuestro.

La señal de la puz

Guía: Alfonso escribió, "La alegría despertó al nacer Jesús y rondaba libre por el mundo." En la alegría del Verbo hecho carne ofrezcámosnos unos a otros una señal del gozo y de la paz navideña.

Rezando con Alfonso en NAVIDAD

Todos se dan una señal de la paz.

◆ 3 ◆
PRAYING WITH ALPHONSUS
IN LENT

Environment: Prominently displayed are a large reproduction of the C.Ss.R. seal and a live plant, surrounded by candles; also a plate on which are enough unsalted almonds to give one to each participant.

Opening Song

"Lord, Who Throughout These Forty Days": *Worship #417*
"The Glory of These Forty Days": *Worship #422*
"Sing, My Tongue, the Song of Triumph": *Worship #437*
"Tree of Life": *Gather Comprehensive #397*

First Reading

Reader 1: A Reading from the Book of the prophet Jeremiah: 1:4–12.

Call to Prayer

Presider: The original seal designed by Saint Alphonsus for the Redemptorist Congregation depicted a large eye looking at the cross. It was intended to illustrate the verse from the prophet Jeremiah that we have just listened to, "I see a branch of the watching tree." In the ancient Near East, the almond tree was nicknamed the "watching tree" because it was the first tree to blossom in spring. It "watched" for the ending of winter and was alert to the motions of new life. For Alphonsus, the cross of Jesus was the true watching tree. The cross heralds the end of the long winter of sin and separation and announces the springtime of new life in relationship with God.

This Lent as we prepare for the celebration of the paschal triduum we pray for the grace of conversion. We pray for the grace to see the world and ourselves with new eyes; with eyes that see life in the midst of death; possibility in the midst of failure; the image and likeness of God in broken humanity. And so we pray.

The presider pauses briefly, and then continues.

Presider: When fear gives way to openness and growth…
All: I see a branch of the watching tree.
Presider: When old quarrels are forgotten and enemies begin to speak to one another…
All: I see a branch of the watching tree.
Presider: When people venture out of their isolation to form community…
All: I see a branch of the watching tree.
Presider: When hidden talents are discovered and creativity flourishes…
All: I see a branch of the watching tree.
Presider: When people have the courage to begin again after failure…
All: I see a branch of the watching tree.

Second Reading

Reader 2: From *The Passion and Death of Jesus Christ* by Saint Alphonsus Liguori: "Jesus, the great high priest, by sacrificing his life for the salvation of his beloved humanity, accomplished the work of the redemption. Jesus Christ, by dying, stripped our death of its terrors. His death makes us worthy to enjoy the same glory that God enjoys and to hear God say one day to us, 'Enter into the joy of your Lord.' …God has more care for us than we have for ourselves. He regards our life as his own riches and our death as his own loss. O how great is our glory while we live in this valley of tears that we are able to say 'We are the Lord's,' we are his possessions."

Steps of the Passion

Presider: Each afternoon, while his brothers were taking their afternoon siesta, Alphonsus would pray the Way of the Cross, which hung in the corridor outside his room. In order not to disturb his resting brothers, Alphonsus would remove his shoes and make the Stations in his bare feet. He reminds us that our devotion to the Passion of Christ should give us tender hearts, full of compassion for human weakness. Alphonsus spent many hours contemplating the Passion of Jesus. He also spent many hours in contemplation of the passion of the poor. We pray now a contemporary adaptation of the *Steps of the Passion of Jesus* written by Saint Alphonsus.

The Steps of the Passion *can be read in turn by different people. Between each of the steps, a Taizé chant is sung, for example, "Jesus, Remember Me" (Gather Comprehensive #404); "Stay Here and Keep Watch" (Gather Comprehensive #411).*

Step I: Loving Jesus, in the garden, your fear was so great that your sweat became like drops of blood; even in such agony you raised your voice in prayer. Loving Jesus, enable us to be the companions of all who are afraid and suffering.

The assembly sings the chosen Taizé chant here and after each of the steps that follow.

Step II: Loving Jesus, you were betrayed by the kiss of a friend, abandoned by your disciples, and taken into custody as a criminal. Loving Jesus, console all those who suffer the pains of broken relationships; console them by your presence *(Taizé chant)*.

Step III: Loving Jesus, you were dragged into court on false charges and were condemned to death. Loving Jesus, give us the courage to denounce injustice. Make us mindful of those in prison, especially those condemned to die *(Taizé chant)*.

Step IV: Loving Jesus, you were stripped of your garments and cruelly beaten. Loving Jesus, make us mindful of those who suffer want because of our indulgence; of those for whom life is cruel and harsh *(Taizé chant)*.

Step V: Loving Jesus, you were crowned with thorns, clothed in a purple robe, and mocked and derided by the soldiers. Loving Jesus, forgive us our persistent prejudices, our mocking of the stranger, our heartless words and cold glances *(Taizé chant)*.

Step VI: Loving Jesus, the thief Barabbas was preferred to you and you were condemned by Pilate to the horrible death of the cross. Loving Jesus, forgive us the suffering we have caused by our indifference, our failures to act, our closing of our eyes and ears to those who suffer *(Taizé chant)*.

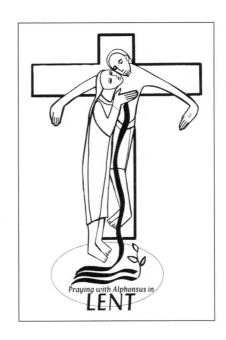

Praying with Alphonsus in
LENT

Step VII: Loving Jesus, you bore the wood of the cross and were lead to your execution like a lamb led to slaughter. Loving Jesus, make us sensitive to those for whom life is a crushing burden and help us to relieve them in their need and lighten their load *(Taizé chant)*.

Step VIII: Loving Jesus, you were nailed on the cross between two thieves, and for three hours endured the terrible torments of the cross. Loving Jesus, make your presence felt by those who are ravaged by disease and who know in their own flesh the torments of the cross (*Taizé chant*).

Step IX: Loving Jesus, your side was pierced by the lance and blood and water flowed out. Loving Jesus, from your open side was born the sacramental life of the church. Make us always grateful for the abundance of life that flowed from your suffering and death (*Taizé chant*).

Step X: Loving Jesus, you were taken from the cross and placed into the arms of your mother. Loving Jesus, console all parents who feel themselves powerless before the sufferings of their children (*Taizé chant*).

Step XI: Loving Jesus, marked by your five wounds, you were anointed for death and placed in the tomb. Loving Jesus, risen from the dead, your wounds are glorious, the sign of love's triumph over death (*Taizé chant*).

Faith-Sharing

The presider initiates faith-sharing by making the following statement:

Presider: In the spirit of the watching tree, share with the person next to you or with the whole group where you see new life in the midst of death in our world today.

Closing Ritual

The presider passes through the assembly the plates of almonds. S/he invites the assembly to keep one almond with them during the rest of the season of Lent, in their pockets or in a place where they can see it often, as a reminder to see the world with new eyes, with the eyes of the watching tree.

Blessing

Presider: As we conclude our prayer, let us make the sign of the cross over one another's eyes that we might look upon the world, one another, and ourselves, with God's own compassion.

3

REZANDO CON ALFONSO EN CUARESMA

Ambiente: En un lugar apropiado se despliega una gran reproducción del sello del C.Ss.R. y una planta viva, rodeada de velas; también un plato en el cual se ponen almendras no saladas suficientes para darle una a cada participante.

Canto de entrada

"Perdón, Oh Dios Mío": *Flor y Canto #110*

Primera Lectura

Lector/a 1: Lectura del libro del profeta Jeremías (Jeremías 1, 4–12).

Llamada a la oración

Guía: El sello original diseñado por San Alfonso para la congregación redentorista representaba un ojo grande mirando a la cruz. Su intención era ilustrar el verso del profeta Jeremías que acabamos de escuchar, "Veo una rama del árbol que llaman 'alerta.'" En el antiguo oriente al almendro se le llamo 'alerta' por ser el primer árbol que florecía en la primavera. El esperaba el fin del invierno y estaba alerta a las señales de nueva vida. Para Alfonso la cruz de Cristo era el verdadero árbol alerta. La cruz anunciaba el fin del largo invierno del pecado y separación y proclamaba la primavera de nueva vida en la relación con Dios.

En esta cuaresma mientras que nos preparamos a celebrar el Triduo Pascual pedimos la gracia de conversión. Rezamos por la gracia de ver el mundo y a nosotros mismos con nuevos ojos, con los ojos que perciben la vida en medio de la muerte; la posibilidad en medio del fracaso; la imagen y semejanza de Dios en la humanidad quebrantada. Y por tanto rezamos…

El guía hace una breve pausa, y continua:

Guía: Cuando el temor se abre al crecimiento…

Todos: Veo una rama del árbol alerta.

Guía: Cuando las viejas contiendas se olvidan y los enemigos comienzan a dialogar…

Todos: Veo una rama del árbol alerta.

Guía: Cuando la gente sale de su aislamiento para formar comunidad…

Todos: Veo una rama del árbol alerta.

Guía: Cuando se descubren talentos escondidos y florece la creatividad…

Todos: Veo una rama del árbol alerta.

Guía: Cuando la gente tiene el coraje de empezar de nuevo después del fracaso…

Todos: Veo una rama del árbol alerta.

Segunda Lectura

Lector/a 2: De la Pasión y Muerte de Jesucristo por San Alfonso Liguori: "Jesús el sumo sacerdote, al sacrificar su vida por la salvación de la humanidad querida, consiguió la obra de la redención. Jesucristo al morir arrancó a nuestra muerte su terror. Su muerte nos hace dignos de disfrutar de la misma gloria de la cual disfruta Dios y oírle decirnos un día, "Entra en el gozo de tu Señor." …Dios cuida de nosotros más de lo que nosotros mismos nos cuidamos. El considera nuestra vida como su propia riqueza y nuestra muerte como su propia pérdida. Oh cuán grande es nuestra gloria mientras vivimos en este valle de lágrimas que podemos decir: "Somos del Señor," somos posesión suya."

Los Pasos de la Pasión

Guía: Cada tarde, mientras sus hermanos tomaban la siesta, Alfonso solía rezar el Vía Crucis que colgaba en el pasillo fuera de su habitación. Para no molestar a sus hermanos que descansaban, Alfonso solía quitarse los zapatos y hacer el Vía Crucis descalzo. Nos recuerda que nuestra devoción a la Pasión de Cristo nos debe enternecer los corazones, llenos de compasión por la debilidad humana. Alfonso pasaba muchas horas contemplando la Pasión de Jesús. También pasaba muchas horas contemplando el sufrimiento de los pobres. Rezamos ahora una adaptación contemporánea de los "Pasos de la Pasión de Jesús," escrita por San Alfonso.

Los Pasos de la Pasión pueden leerse por turno por diferentes personas. Entre cada uno de los Pasos se canta un canto de Taizé, por ejemplo: Jesús, Recuérdame.

I: Amante Jesús, en el jardín tu temor fue tan grande, que tu sudor se hizo gotas de sangre; aún en tal agonía elevaste tu voz en oración. Amante Jesús, ház que seamos compañeros de todos los que tienen miedo y sufren.

La asamblea canta el canto elegido ahora y despúes de cada reflexión.

II: Amante Jesús, fuiste traicionado por el beso de un amigo, abandonado por tus discípulos, y arrestado como un criminal. Amante Jesús, conforta a todos los que sufren los dolores de relaciones quebradas; confórtalos con tu presencia *(canto)*.

III: Amante Jesús, fuiste arrastrado a la corte bajo cargos falsos y fuiste condenado a muerte. Amante Jesús, dános fortaleza para denunciar injusticias. Háznos conscientes de los encarcelados, especialmente de los condenados a pena de muerte *(canto)*.

IV: Amante Jesús, te fueron arrancados tus vestidos y fuiste cruelmente apaleado. Amante Jesús, háznos conscientes de los que sufren por causa de nuestra indulgencia; de aquellos por quienes la vida es cruel y dura *(canto)*.

V: Amante Jesús, fuiste coronado de espinas, vestido de una bata morada y mofado e insultado por los soldados. Amante Jesús, perdona nuestros prejuicios, nuestra mofa del extranjero, nuestras palabras duras y nuestras miradas frías *(canto)*.

VI: Amante Jesús, el homicida Barrabás fue preferido a tí y fuiste condenado por Pilato a la muerte horrible de la cruz. Amante Jesús, perdónanos el sufrimiento que hemos causado por nuestra indiferencia, por dejar de actuar, por cerrar los ojos y los oídos hacia los que sufren *(canto)*.

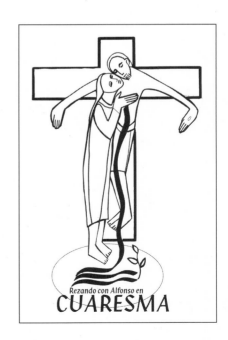

VII: Amante Jesús, cargaste con el leño de la cruz y fuiste conducido a tu ejecución como cordero llevado al matadero. Amante Jesús, háznos sensibles hacia aquellos para quienes la vida es una carga aplastante y ayúdanos a aliviarlos en su necesidad y a aligerar su carga *(canto)*.

VIII: Amante, Jesús, fuiste clavado en la cruz entre dos ladrones, y por tres horas soportaste los terribles tormentos de la cruz. Amante Jesús, ház que se sienta tu presencia por aquellos que son asolados por la enfermedad y que conocen en su carne los tormentos de la cruz *(canto)*.

IX: Amante Jesús, tu costado fue traspasado por la lanza y corrió sangre y agua. Amante Jesús, de tu costado abierto nació la vida sacramental de la Iglesia, háznos siempre agradecidos por la abundancia de vida que fluyó de tus sufrimientos y muerte *(canto)*.

X: Amante Jesús, fuiste bajado de la cruz y puesto en brazos de tu madre. Amante Jesús, consuela a todos los padres que se sienten impotentes ante los sufrimientos de sus hijos *(canto)*.

XI: Amante Jesús, marcado por tus cinco heridas, fuiste ungido para la muerte y colocado en la tumba. Amante, Jesús, resucitado de entre los muertos, gloriosas son tus heridas, señal del triunfo del amor sobre la muerte *(canto)*.

Compartiendo la fe

Guía: En el espíritu del árbol que se llama alerta, comparte con la persona al lado tuyo o con el grupo entero, ¿dónde ves tú nueva vida en medio de la muerte hoy en el mundo?

Ritual

El guía pasa por la asamblea los platos de almendras. Les invita a que conserven una consigo durante el resto de la cuaresma, en los bolsillos o en un lugar donde la podrán ver con frecuencia, como recordatorio para ver al mundo con nuevos ojos, con los ojos del alerce.

Bendición

Guía: Mientras se termina nuestra oración hagamos la señal de la cruz sobre cada uno de los ojos de los demás a fin de ver el mundo, unos a otros y a nosotros mismos, con la misma compasión de Dios.

PRAYING WITH ALPHONSUS AT EASTER

Environment: The participants are seated in a circle. In the center of the room are the paschal candle or another large candle, two smaller candles which are lighted before the beginning of the prayer service, and a basket containing pieces of bread, enough for each participant to have a piece.

Opening Song

"Gospel Acclamation," Mass of Creation: *Gather Comprehensive* #160

Invitation to Prayer

Presider: For Alphonsus, the Risen Jesus lives forever among us in the Eucharist, meeting us as did the disciples on the road to Emmaus, in the breaking of the bread. Alphonsus writes, "Those who receive the Eucharist abide in Jesus and Jesus in them. This union is…a true and real union. As the flames of two wax tapers when joined unite themselves into one so we in the Eucharist become one with Jesus."

Two members of the assembly stand, each takes one of the smaller candles and together they light the paschal candle, and then extinguish the smaller candles.

Readings

Reader 1: This is a reading from the Gospel of Luke: 24:13–24.
All: In response to the reading, the assembly sings the "Gospel Acclamation" from above: "Alleluia, Alleluia, praise the word of truth and love."
Reader 2: This is a reading from the Gospel of Luke: 24:25-27.
All: The assembly sings the "Gospel Acclamation."
Reader 3: This is a reading from the Gospel of Luke: 24:28-35.
All: The assembly sings the "Gospel Acclamation."

Pause for Silent Reflection

Faith-Sharing

Presider: *The presider asks the assembly to break up into pairs just as the disciples did on the road to Emmaus. The presider reads each of the following questions and asks that each pair share their reflections on these questions:*

When have I experienced my heart burning within me when I heard the Word of God proclaimed or preached? Name an experience that has been "eucharist" for you.

Ritual of Sharing Bread

Presider: Jesus broke the word of the Scriptures for us.
All: And our hearts burned within us.
Presider: We have met the Lord Jesus.
All: In the breaking of the bread.
Presider: The Lord is risen, Alleluia.
All: He is risen indeed, Alleluia.
Presider: Let us pray. God our Creator, you who have made the heavens and the earth, have become a companion at our table. Your Word, who formed the universe, has burned like a fire in our hearts. Your life-giving Spirit sends us forth with power to proclaim the triumph of love in our broken world. Bless this bread which we share in your name. In sharing it with one another, may we recognize your presence. As we walk together on the way, may we met you, our beloved companion, Jesus the Wayfarer, our Redeemer.

The basket of bread is passed. Each person takes a piece, passes the bread to the next person, and says, "We have met the Lord…" to which the person responds, "in the breaking of the bread."

Closing Song

Presider: We conclude our prayer in song, rejoicing with Mary and all of creation for the abundance of life that is the Risen Redeemer's gift to us.

The assembly sings "Regina Caeli Laetare" ("O Queen of Heaven"): Worship Comprehensive #447.

Blessing

Presider: *Peace* was the first word of the Risen Jesus to his disciples. Let us offer to one another a sign of Easter peace.

The assembly offers one another the sign of peace.

REZANDO CON ALFONSO EN PASCUA DE RESURRECCIÓN

Ambiente: Los participantes están sentados en un círculo, de ser posible alrededor de una mesa o mesas. En el centro del cuarto donde tiene lugar la oración se colocan el cirio pascual, otro cirio grande, dos velas pequeñas ya encendidas al comienzo de la oración, y un cesto con trozos de pan, suficientes para que cada participante tenga un trozo.

Canto de entrada

"Resucitó": *Flor y Canto #152*

Invitación a orar

Guía: Para Alfonso, Jesús resucitado vive siempre entre nosotros en la eucaristía. Como los discípulos en el camino de Emaús, Alfonso se encontró con Jesús en la fracción del pan. Alfonso escribe, "Aquellos que reciben la eucaristía moran en Jesús y Jesús en ellos. Esta unión no es sólo una de afecto, pero una unión verdadera y real. Como las llamas de dos velas de cera cuando se juntan se unen como una, así nosotros en la eucaristía nos hacemos uno con Jesús."

Dos miembros de la asamblea se ponen de pie, cada uno toma una de las velas pequeñas y juntos encienden el cirio pascual, y apagan las velas pequeñas.

Lecturas

Lector/a 1: Lucas 24, 13–24.
Todos: Todos cantan el refrán como arriba, "Aleluya, Aleluya."
Lector/a 2: Lucas 24, 25–27.
Todos: Todos cantan el refrán como arriba, "Aleluya, Aleluya."
Lector/a 3: Lucas 24, 28–35.
Todos: Tosos cantan el refrán como arriba, "Aleluya, Aleluya."

Una pausa para orar en silencio

Compartir la fe

Guía: Como los discípulos, camino de Emaús, la asamblea se divide en pares y comparte unos con otros sus reflecciones sobre una o ambas de estas preguntas:

¿Cuándo he experimentado que me ardía el corazón por dentro al escuchar la palabra de Dios proclamada o predicada? Menciona una experiencia que ha sido "eucaristía" para tí.

Ritual de compartir el Pan

Guía: Jesús partió la palabra de las escrituras para nosotros.

Todos: Y ardían nuestros corazones.

Guía: Hemos encontrado al Señor Jesús.

Todos: En la fracción del pan.

Guía: Ha resucitado el Señor, Aleluya.

Todos: Ha resucitado de verdad, Aleluya.

Guía: Dios creador nuestro, tú que has hecho los cielos y la tierra, te has hecho compañero en nuestra mesa. Tu palabra que formó el universo ha ardido como fuego en nuestros corazones. Tu Espíritu vivificante nos envía con el poder de proclamar el triunfo del amor en nuestro mundo quebrantado. Bendice este pan que compartimos en tu nombre. Mientras lo compartimos entre nosotros que reconzcamos tu presencia. Mientras caminamos juntos, que te encontremos, nuestro querido compañero, Jesús el Caminante, nuestro Redentor.

Se pasa el cesto de pan. Cada persona toma un pedazo, pasa el pan a la próxima persona y dice, "Hemos encontrado al Señor…" a lo cual responde la persona, "en la fracción del pan."

Canción Final

Guía: Concluímos nuestra oración con un canto, regocijándonos con María y con toda la creación por la abundancia de vida que es el don del Redentor resucitado a nosotros.

Todos: Todos cantan: Regina Coeli Laetare.

CANTICOS de Gracias y Alabanza #170 Adios, Reina del Cielo.

Bendición

Guía: "La paz" fue la primera palabra de Jesús resucitado a sus discípulos. Ofrezcamos uno a otro una señal de la paz de Pascua.

PRAYING WITH ALPHONSUS
AT PENTECOST

Environment: Symbols of the four elements, each of which Alphonsus uses as symbols for the action of the Holy Spirit, are placed in a prominent location: For earth, a bowl of soil; for air, a bowl of burning incense, a feather, wind chimes; for fire, a candle or an oil lamp; for water, an attractive vessel of water. Also slips of paper, a sufficient number according to the number of participants, on which are written Alphonsus's reflections on the gifts of the Holy Spirit.

Opening Song

"Veni Creator Spiritus": *Worship* #479
"Come Holy Ghost": *Worship* #482
"The Spirit of God": *Gather Comprehensive* #458

Call to Prayer

Presider: Saint Alphonsus painted a picture of Our Lady of the Holy Spirit. It depicts Mary dressed as an ordinary, peasant woman. In the picture, as Mary lifts her veil from her chest, the radiant dove of the Holy Spirit is seen there. As we begin our prayer, let us place a hand over our hearts and honor the presence of the Holy Spirit within us. *(All pray in silence for a few moments.)*

Presider: Let's turn to a person next to us and place a hand on his/her chest as he/she places one on ours and pray in silence to reverence the presence of the Spirit in each other.

Presider: Let us call forth the presence of the Holy Spirit on our gathering in the words of the prayer of Saint Alphonsus:

Most Holy Spirit, the Consoler, Defender of the Poor, Comfort of the afflicted, light of our hearts, God's holy presence in our souls; come and make us aware of your presence. Your presence fills us with holy reverence. We bless you a thousand times and with the seraphim who stand before your throne we also sing:

All: *The assembly sings any well-known version of the acclamation "Holy, Holy, Holy…"*

Response

Presider: You made Mary full of grace and you inflamed the hearts of the apostles with a holy zeal.

All: Inflame our hearts with your love.

Presider: You are the Spirit of Goodness.

All: Give us the courage to confront evil.

Presider: You are Fire.

All: Set us ablaze with your love.

Presider: You are Light.

All: Enlighten our minds that we may see what is truly important.

Presider: You are the Dove.

All: Give us gentleness.

Presider: You are a Soothing Breeze.

All: Bring calm to the storms that rage within us.

Presider: You are the Tongue.

All: May our lips ever sing God's praises.

Presider: You are the Cloud.

All: Shelter us under the shadow of your protection.

Readings

Reader 1: This is a reading from Acts of the Apostles: 2:14–21, 41–47.

Pause for Silent Reflection

Reader 2: A reading from the Novena to the Holy Spirit by Saint Alphonsus:

The Church teaches us to pray: "May the Holy Spirit inflame us with that fire which Jesus came to cast on the earth and which he ardently desired to set ablaze." This was the holy fire which inflamed the saints to do great things for God, to love their enemies, to be unconcerned with reputation, to live indifferent to material things, to embrace any discomfort and even death itself with delight. Love cannot remain idle. Love never says, "Enough!" The person who loves God, the more she does for her beloved, the more she desires to do. This holy fire is enkindled by prayer. As psalmist says, "In my meditation a fire shall flame out." If we desire to burn with love toward God, let us love prayer. Prayer is the furnace in which divine love is enkindled.

Pause for Silent Reflection

Ritual

After the silent reflection the presider invites the participants to come forward and pick a slip of paper on which is written Alphonsus's description on one of the gifts of the Holy Spirit. The presider invites the group to a period of silent prayer in which each participant first prays for that gift for him/herself and them formulates a petition for the outpouring of that gift of the Spirit on the group which will be spoken aloud in the period of intercessory prayer that follows.

Pause for Silent Reflection

Intercessions

Presider: Sharing Saint Alphonsus's confidence that God lavishes the Spirit's gifts upon the world in abundance, let us pray for an outpouring of the Spirit's gifts on ourselves and our community:

Each person formulates a petition on the gift of the Spirit on his or her slip of paper. To each petition all respond, "Come, Holy Spirit!"

Presider: *Fear of the Lord:* This gift prevents us from falling into our former patterns of sinfulness and inspires us to ask God for pardon and strength.

Responder: Answers with a petition based on the gift of fear of the Lord.

All: Come, Holy Spirit.

Presider: *Piety:* This gift gives us enthusiasm in God's service, inspires us to follow God's holy inspirations with greater promptness, and to follow the way of God's commandments with greater fidelity.

Responder: Answers with a petition based on the gift of piety.

All: Come, Holy Spirit

Presider: *Knowledge:* This gift gives us deeper insight into the things of God and enables us to walk steadily in the way of salvation.

Responder: Answers with a petition based on the gift of knowledge.

All: Come, Holy Spirit.

Presider: *Fortitude:* This gift gives us courage to resists the enticements of evil and gives us the energy to avoid anything that might impede my relationship with God.

Responder: Offers a petition based on the gift of fortitude.

All: Come, Holy Spirit.

Presider: *Counsel:* This gift enables us to make good choices in life; to discern in times of doubt and confusion how to choose what is most conducive to my well-being and that of others.

Responder: Offers a petition based on the gift of counsel.

All: Come, Holy Spirit.

Presider: Understanding: This gift enables us to distinguish between what is really important in life and what is a deceptive illusion.

Responder: Offers a petition based on the gift of understanding.

All: Come, Holy Spirit.

Presider: *Wisdom:* This gift enables us to direct all our actions to God as our truest good and to serve and love God as we ought so as to live forever in the possession of love.

Responder: Offers a petition based on the gift of wisdom.

All: Come, Holy Spirit.

Final Blessing

Four members of the group each hold aloft one of the symbols of the four elements while the presider prays the prayer of blessing:

Presider: Holy Spirit, you give life and growth to our earth. Fill us with gratitude for God's abundant gifts.

All: Amen!

Presider: Holy Spirit, in the beginning, you moved over the waters to bring creation out of chaos. Move within us to give us lives of wholeness and integrity.

All: Amen!

Presider: Holy Spirit, you come as a mighty wind that shakes the foundations of our world. Be our energy to build God's reign.

All: Amen!

Presider: Holy Spirit, who came at Pentecost as tongues of fire. Make us fearless apostles of the gospel of Jesus.

All: Amen!

PENTECOST

Praying with Alphonsus in

5

REZANDO CON ALFONSO EN PENTECOSTÉS

Ambiente: Símbolos de los cuatro elementos, cada uno de los cuales utiliza Alfonso como símbolos de la acción del Espíritu Santo, se colocan en un lugar apropiado: tierra: una fuente de tierra; aire: una fuente de incienso ardiente/una pluma de ave/un juego de campanillas; fuego: una vela o lámpara de aceite; agua: una vasija atractiva de agua. Además, pedacitos de papel, en número suficiente según los participantes, en los que se escriben las reflecciones de Alfonso sobre los dones del Espíritu Santo.

Canto de entrada

"Espíritu Santo Ven": *Flor y Canto #174,*

Invitar a orar

Guía: San Alfonso dibujó un cuadro de Nuestra Señora del Espíritu Santo. Pinta a María vestida como una mujer campesina corriente. Ella eleva el velo de su pecho y se ve ahí la paloma radiante del Espíritu Santo. Al comenzar nuestra oración, pongamos la mano sobre nuestros corazones y honremos la presencia del Espíritu Santo dentro de nosotros. (*Todos rezan en silencio por unos momentos.*)

Guía: Veamos hacia la persona al lado de nosotros y pongamos la mano sobre su pecho mientras él/ella nos pone la mano sobre el nuestro y oremos en silencio para reverenciar la presencia del Espíritu el uno en el otro.

Guía: Invoquemos la presencia del Espíritu Santo sobre nuestra asamblea con las palabras de la oración de San Alfonso:

Santísimo Espíritu, Consolador, defensor de los Pobres, Consuelo de los afligidos, luz de nuestros corazones, presencia sagrada de Dios en nuestras almas, ven y háznos conscientes de tu presencia. Tu presencia nos llena de santa reverencia. Te bendecimos mil veces y con los serafines que están de pie alrededor de tu trono también cantamos:

Todos: *Santo, Santo, Santo…* (se canta cualquier versión bien conocida de esta aclamación.)

Respuesta

Guía: Tú colmaste a María de gracia e inflamaste los corazones de los apóstoles con santo celo.

Todos: Enciende nuestros corazones con tu amor.

Guía: Tú eres el Espíritu de Bondad.

Todos: Dános el coraje de enfrentarnos con el mal.

Guía: Tú eres fuego.

Todos: Enciende en nosotros la llama de tu amor.

Guía: Tú eres Luz.

Todos: Ilumina nuestras mentes para que apreciemos lo que tiene verdadera importancia.

Guía: Tú eres la Paloma.

Todos: Dános mansedumbre.

Guía: Tú eres una Brisa Dulce.

Todos: Calma las tormentas furiosas en nosotros.

Guía: Tú eres la Lengua.

Todos: Que nuestros labios siempre canten las alabanzas de Dios.

Guía: Tú eres la Nube.

Todos: Cobíjanos bajo la sombra de tu protección.

Lecturas

Lector/a 1: Hechos 2, 14–21. 41–47.

Una pausa para orar en silencio

Lector/a 2: Lectura de la Novena al Santo Espíritu por San Alfonso: "La Iglesia nos enseña a rezar: 'Que el Espíritu Santo nos inflame con el fuego que Jesús vino a derramar en la tierra y tan ardientemente quiso encender.' Este fue el fuego santo que encendía a los santos a fin de que hicieran cosas grandes para Dios, amar a sus enemigos, ser indiferente al que dirán, vivir indiferente a las cosas materiales, abrasar cualquier incomodidad y aún la misma muerte con deleite. El amor no puede permanecer desocupado. El amor núnca dice '¡Basta!' La persona que ama a Dios, cuanto más haga por su amado tanto más desea hacer. Este fuego santo se enciende por la oración. Como dice el salmista: "En mi meditación arderá un fuego." Si deseamos arder con amor hacia Dios, amemos la oración. La oración es el horno en donde se enciende el amor divino.

Una pausa para orar en silencio

Ritual

Después de la reflexión en silencio el presidente invita a los participantes a que se acerquen y tomen un pedacito de papel en que está escrito la reseña de Alfonso sobre unos de los dones del Espíritu Santo. El guía invita al grupo a pasar un período de oración en silencio en el cual cada participante pide primero por ese don por sí mismo; y luego compone una petición por la efusión de ese don del Espíritu sobre el grupo, la cual se dirá en voz alta en el período de oración intercesora que sigue.

Una pausa para orar en silencio

Intercesiones

Guía: Ya que compartimos la confianza de San Alfonso que Dios derrocha los dones del Espíritu sobre el mundo en abundancia, oremos por una efusión de los dones del Espíritu sobre nosotros y sobre nuestra comunidad:

Cada persona compone una petición sobre el don del Espíritu en su pedazo de papel. A cada petición todos responden: Ven Espíritu Santo.

Guía: Temor del Señor: Este don nos impide recaer en nuestras actuaciones anteriores de pecado y nos inspira a pedirle a Dios perdón y fortaleza.

Respuesta: Responde con una petición por el don de Temor de Dios.

Todos: Ven Espíritu Santo.

Guía: Piedad: Este don nos da entusiasmo en el servicio de Dios, nos impulsa a seguir las santas inspiraciones de Dios con más prontitud, y a seguir los caminos de los mandamientos de Dios con más fidelidad.

Respuesta: Responde con una petición por el don de Piedad.

Todos: Ven Espíritu Santo.

Guía: Ciencia: Este don nos hace penetrar más profundamente en las cosas de Dios y nos habilita a caminar firmemente en las sendas de la salvación.

Respuesta: Responde con una petición por el don de Fortaleza.

Todos: Ven Espíritu Santo.

Guía: Fortaleza: Este don nos da coraje para resistir las seducciones del mal y nos da la energía para evitar cualquier cosa que pueda impedir mi relación con Dios.

Respuesta: Answers with a petition based on the gift of fortitude.

Todos: Ven Espíritu Santo.

Guía: Consejo: Este don nos habilita a tomar buenas decisiones para vivir bien; a discernir en tiempo de dudas y confusión el cómo escoger lo que más conduce a nuestro bienestar y el de los demás.

Respuesta: Responde con una petición por el don de Consejo.

Todos: Ven Espíritu Santo.

Guía: Inteligencia: Este don nos permite distinguir entre lo que realmente es importante en la vida y lo que es ilusión engañosa.

Respuesta: Responde con una petición por el don de Inteligencia.

Todos: Ven Espíritu Santo.

Guía: Sabiduría: Este don nos hablita a dirigir todas mis acciones hacia Dios como a mi bien más verdadero y a servir y amar a Dios como debo a fin de vivir para siempre en la posesión del amor.

Respuesta: Responde con una petición por el don de Sabiduría.

Todos: Ven Espíritu Santo.

Bendición final

Cuatro miembros del grupo elevan uno de los símbolos de los cuatro elementos mientras el presidente reza la siguiente oración:

Guía: Espíritu Santo, tú das vida y crecimiento a nuestra tierra. Llénanos con gratitud por los dones abundantes de Dios.

Todos: ¡Amén!

Guía: Espíritu Santo, en el principio, te moviste sobre las aguas para sacar la creación del caos. Actúa en nosotros a fin de darnos vidas de salud e integridad.

Todos: ¡Amén!

Guía: Espíritu Santo, vienes como viento poderoso que sacude los cimientos de nuestro mundo. Sé nuestra energía para edificar el reino de Dios.

Todos: ¡Amén!

Guía: Espíritu Santo, que viniste en Pentecostés a manera de lenguas de fuego. Háznos apóstoles valientes del evangelio de Jesús.

Todos: ¡Amén!

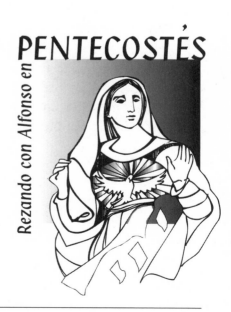

Rezando con Alfonso en PENTECOSTÉS

PRAYING WITH ALPHONSUS
IN ORDINARY TIME

Environment: On a cloth and surrounded by candles and flowers can be placed ordinary objects symbolic of daily life: pots and pans, tools, car keys, datebooks, pens and pencils, and so on.

Call to Prayer

Presider: Between the times of feast and fast, the Church year gives us large portions of "ordinary time."

"Ordinary time" is an opportunity to savor the presence of God in the routine, in the average, in the everyday. Its sacred places are the kitchen, the living room, the office, the supermarket, the factory. Its sacred ministers are the people closest to us—our family, friends, our coworkers, our intimates, and also our enemies. It is a time to have our feet on the ground, our sleeves rolled up, the coffeepot always ready for hospitality.

Alphonsus never taught a particular "devotion," but he was very concerned with teaching ordinary people how to live a "*vita devota*," a devout life—a life in which all our activities were acts of praise and thanksgiving to God. Let us begin our prayer by raising our voices in a song of praise to our God who does not reserve his power and presence to special times and places but who loves us always and everywhere, in the most seemingly ordinary times.

Opening Song

"Lord of All Hopefulness": *Worship* #568
"For the Beauty of the Earth": *Gather Comprehensive* #572
"Center of My Life": *Gather Comprehensive* #598

First Reading and Response

Reader 1: From *The Way to Converse With God As a Friend* by Saint Alphonsus: "When your eye rests on scenes in the country or along the shore, or flowers, or fruits, and you are delighted by the sight or scent of it all, say to yourself, 'Look how creation is filled with God's beauty! And all these things were made to draw me to God's love. If earth is so beautiful, what must the reign of God be like?' When you see rivers or brooks, reflect that just as the water which you see keeps running on to the ocean without ever stopping, so ought you to be running toward God, your greatest good. When you see a puppy, which is so faithful to its master just for a little bit of food, think how much more reason you have to be faithful to God who heaps such abundance on you. When you hear the birds sing you, too, should praise God with acts of love as they do. When you see a beautifully ornamented church, remember that the human being in the state of God's grace is the truest temple of God. When you look up at the sky, all studded with stars, say, 'O my feet, God has made them a pathway for you!'"

Different speakers respond to the reading with the words of Psalm 27. The presider appoints those who will read.

Speaker 1: The Lord is my light and my salvation; I need not fear anything.

Speaker 2: The Lord upholds my life; what could possibly threaten me?

Speaker 3: Even if my enemies advance like wild beasts,
       I trust that God would rout them.

Speaker 4: Surrounded by an army, my heart is fearless.

Speaker 5: Even if war rages around me, even then would I trust.

Speaker 6: One thing I ask from the Lord, for this I long.

Speaker 7: To live at home in God's house all the days of my life.

Speaker 8: I wish to delight my eyes with God's beauty, to rest in God's dwelling.

Speaker 9: God shelters me in time of trouble.

Speaker 10: God nestles me within a tent.

Speaker 11: God sets me high on a rock.

Speaker 12: I hold my head high before those who threaten me.

Speaker 13: With ringing voice I offer sacrifice in the holy temple, with shouts of joy.

Speaker 14: I will sing, I will chant the praises of my God!

Second Reading and Response

Reader 2: This is a reading from *The Way to Converse With God As a Friend* by Saint Alphonsus Liguori: "Your whole life long, may God be your only happiness, the only object of your affections, the only end of your actions and desires. You will come one day to that world without end, where your love will be in every way perfected and completed. Your desires will be perfectly fulfilled and completely satisfied."

Presider: We respond in words of Alphonsus, about which he said, "Whoever says this little canticle from the heart causes joy in paradise."

All: Jesus, my true, my only love,
I wish for nothing but you.
Here I am, I am yours, my God.
Do what you will with me.

Pause for Silent Prayer

Faith-Sharing

Presider: Share with a person next to you, or with the entire group, an experience of becoming aware of the presence of God in the circumstances of daily life; a time when an ordinary object or event made you very conscious of God's presence or action.

Ritual

At the end of the period of silent prayer or of faith-sharing, the presider passes a basket in which are papers each of which contains a suggestion recommended by Saint Alphonsus for living the activities of daily life in a spirit of devotion. Each person takes one and resolves to try to practice it at the appropriate time for the coming week. These practices are listed in the box on pages 38–39. These suggestions may be copied and cut up so that there are a sufficient number of suggestions for the number of people in the group.

Intercessions

Presider: Our world is flawed yet richly graced. Let us present its needs to the mercy of God.

All: Fill our days with your peace.

Presider: We ask God's blessing on our rising and our going to rest, on our labors and pleasures, on our silence and on our speech.

All: Fill our days with your peace.

Presider: May all those we love, our families, relatives and friends, know our concern for them and experience our concern in words and actions of love.

All: Fill our days with your peace.

Presider: May our whole life, even during moments of routine and boredom, be filled with a sense of God's presence and providence.

All: Fill our days with your peace.

Presider: For those who experience life as a burden, the depressed, the abandoned, the sick.

All: Fill our days with your peace.

Presider: For those who have finished their earthly course of days and live in God's eternal present.

All: Fill our days with your peace.

Presider: Let us invite members of this assembly to offer additional spontaneous petitions to which we will answer, "Fill our days with your peace."

The Our Father

Presider: Let us join our voices in the prayers that we first learned from those we love and to which are the nourishing daily bread of our prayer:

All: *The assembly says the Our Father in unison.*

The Hail Mary

Presider: We share the confidence of Saint Alphonsus that Mary accompanies us during the days of our lives and the hour of our death, so we pray:

All: *The assembly says the Hail Mary in unison.*

Blessing

Presider: We conclude our prayer by marking ourselves with the sign of our redemption in Christ.

All: In the name of the Father, and of the Son, and of the Holy Spirit. Amen.

RECOMMENDATIONS
FOR LIVING A DEVOUT LIFE

Place something beautiful (a flower, a piece of fruit, a photo of someone you love) near your bed where you can see it when you awaken. Praise God for these gifts.

Make in the morning an agreement with God that every time you make a certain sign such as placing your hand on your heart you wish thereby to make an act of love for God and a desire to see God loved by everyone.

Breathe deeply and invite the Holy Spirit, breath of God, into your heart.

When you hear the phone ring, pause for a moment to recall the presence of God in the person who is calling before you answer it.

Drink a glass of water slowly and be aware that from all eternity God was creating that gift of water for your refreshment.

Spend a few moments several times today reading Scripture, remembering, as Alphonsus said, that there is nothing better able to enkindle the love of God in us than the word of God found in Scripture.

Choose a few words of Scripture and repeat them often during the day. Alphonsus says, "One holy sentence, well chewed, is enough to make us saints."

When you get dressed, find something in your closet that you really don't need and give it to someone who does.

Alphonsus and his companions used to place food to be given to the poor at the feet of a statue of the Infant Jesus during every meal. Skip a meal this week and send the money to an organization that feeds hungry children.

Take a walk and praise God for each of the beautiful things you see.

Buy or borrow a life of a saint to read and make that person your companion through the week.

Recall that each person you met today is the true dwelling place of God. Make an act of spiritual communion with the presence of Jesus in them.

Pause at morning, noon, and evening, to place your hand on your heart and recall the coming of God in human flesh.

Think of Alphonsus at his harpsichord while you delight in listening to a favorite piece of music.

Buy a special candle that you will light for a few moments every Thursday evening to recall the great gift God has given us in the institution of the Eucharist.

On Saturdays, donate some time to a work of justice and peace in honor of Mary, the Woman of Mercy.

In order to call to mind frequently the mysteries of our Savior's love, when you see hay, a manger, a cave, let the Infant Jesus in the stable of Bethlehem be present to your imagination.

In order to call to mind frequently the mysteries of our Savior's love, when you see a saw, a hammer, a plane, or an ax, remember the life of humble labor lived by our Savior in Nazareth.

In order to call to mind frequently the mysteries of our Savior's love, when you see ropes, thorns, nails, or pieces of wood, reflect on the Passion and Death of our Redeemer.

In order to call to mind frequently the mysteries of our Savior's love, whenever you see bread, grapes, wine, or any vessels for eating, recall to mind the greatness of love which Jesus has for us in giving us the sacrament of the Eucharist.

As often as you can throughout the day repeat the prayer, "O God, come to my assistance. O Lord, make haste to help me."

As often as you can throughout the day repeat as a prayer the names of Jesus and Mary.

REZANDO CON ALFONSO EN EL TIEMPO ORDINARIO

Ambiente: En un mantel y rodeado de velas y flores se pueden colocar objetos ordinarios que simbolizan la vida diaria: casuelas y sarténes, herramientas, llaves del auto, libro de fechas, cuadernos y lápices, etc.

Llamado a la oración

Guía: Entre los tiempos de fiesta y ayuno, el año liturgico nos proporciona largos períodos de "tiempo ordinario." "El tiempo ordinario" nos da la oportunidad de saborear la presencia de Dios en la rutina, en lo corriente, en lo ordinario. Sus lugares sagrados son la cocina, la sala, la oficina, el supermercado, la factoría. Sus ministros sagrados son las personas más cercanas—nuestra familia, nuestros compañeros de trabajo, nuestros amigos íntimos, como también los enemigos. Es una ocasión de poner los pies en la tierra, las mangas recogidas, y el café siempre listo para mostrar hospitalidad.

Alfonso núnca enseñó una 'devoción' particular pero sí se afanaba de enseñarle a la gente ordinaria cómo llevar un 'vita devota,' una vida de "devoción" una vida en la cual todas nuestras actividades fueran actos de alabanza y acción de gracias a Dios. Comencemos elevando nuestras voces en un canto de alabanza a Dios que no conserva su poder ni su presencia para momentos y lugares especiales sino que nos ama siempre y en todo lugar, en los momentos más insignificantes.

Canto de entrada

"Tu Palabra Me Da Vida": *Flor y Canto* #563

Primera Lectura

Lector/a 1: De La Manera de Conversar Con Dios como Con Un Amigo por San Alfonso:
"Cuando descansan tus ojos en escenas del campo o de la costa, o de flores o frutas, y te deleitas con la vista o el olor de todo ésto, dí para tí mismo: "¡Mira cómo la

creación está llena de la belleza de Dios! Y todas estas cosas fueron creadas para atraerme al amor de Dios. Si la tierra es tan bella, ¡Cómo será el reino de Dios? Cuando miras los ríos o los riachuelos, considera que así como las aguas que ves siguen corriendo hacia el oceano sin jamás parar, así debes tú correr hacia Dios, tu bien supremo. Cuando ves un cachorro, que es tan fiel a su maestro sólo por una migaja de comida, considera cuánta más razón tienes de mantenerte fiel a Dios que te colma de tanta abundancia. Cuando oyes cantar a los pájaros tú también debes alabar a Dios con actos de amor como hacen ellos. Cuando ves una iglesia bellamente adornada, recuerda que el ser humano en estado de gracia es el más verdadero templo de Dios. Cuando miras el cielo todo adornado de estrellas, dí, ¡Oh pies míos, Dios los ha hecho un sendero para tí!"

Salmo Responsorial

Guía: Rezamos con las palabras del salmo 26, cada persona dice un versículo por turno.

Lector/a 1: El Señor es mi luz y mi salvación, ¿a quién temeré?

Lector/a 2: El Señor es la defensa de mi vida, ¿quién me hará temblar?

Lector/a 3: Cuando me asaltan los malvados,para devorar mi carne, mis enemigos y adversarios, tropiezan y caen.

Lector/a 4: Acorralado por un ejército, mi corazón no tiembla.

Lector/a 5: Si me declaran la guerra, me siento tranquilo.

Lector/a 6: Una cosa pido al Señor, eso buscaré;

Lector/a 7: Habitar en la casa del Señor por los días de mi vida.

Lector/a 8: Gozar de la dulzura del Señor contemplando su templo.

Lector/a 9: El me protegerá en su tienda.

Lector/a 10: En el día de peligro me esconderé en el escondite de su morada.

Lector/a 11: Me alzará sobre la roca.

Lector/a 12: Y así levantaré la cabeza sobre el enemigo que me cerca.

Lector/a 13: En su tienda sacrificaré sacrificios de aclamación.

Lector/a 14: Cantaré y tocaré para el Señor.

Segunda Lectura y Respuesta

Lector/a 2: De La Manera de Conversar Con Dios como Con Un Amigo por San Alfonso: "Qué en toda tu vida sea Dios tu única felicidad, el único objeto de tus afectos, el único fin de tus acciones y anhelos. Llegarás algún día a ese mundo sin fin, donde tu amor será perfecto y completo en todos modos. Serán tus deseos perfectamente realizados y completamente satisfechos."

Responsorio

Guía: Respondemos con las palabras de Alfonso, de las cuales dijo él, "Cualquiera que diga este cántico pequeño de corazón causa alegría en el paraíso:"

Todos: Jesús, mi verdadero, mi único amor,

Deseo nada sino a tí.

Aquí me tienes, soy tuyo, Dios mío,

Ház lo que quieras conmigo.

Una pausa para orar en silencio

Compartiendo la fe

Guía: Comparte con la persona al lado tuyo, o con el grupo entero, una experiencia en que te hiciste consciente de la presencia de Dios en tu vida ordinaria; un momento en que un objeto corriente o un evento te hizo muy consciente de la presencia o la acción de Dios.

Ritual

Al final del período de oración en silencio o de compartir la fe, el presidente pasa un cesto en que hay papeles que tienen sugerencias recomendadas por San Alfonso para realizar las actividades de la vida diaria con espíritu de devoción. Cada persona toma uno y resuelve procurar de practicarla en el momento oportuno durante la semana que viene. (Vea el Apéndice; se puede copiar y cortar la página a fin de que haya suficiente número de sugerencias según el número de las personas en el grupo.)

Intercesiones

Guía: Nuestro mundo es a la vez defectuoso y abundantemente embellecido. Presentemos nuestras necesidades a la misericordia de Dios.

Todos: Llena nuestros días de tu paz.

Guía: Imploramos la bendición de Dios al levantarnos y al acostarnos, sobre nuestras labores y placeres, sobre nuestro silencio y nuestro hablar….

Todos: Llena nuestros días de tu paz.

Guía: Que sepan todos los que amamos, nuestras familias, parientes y amigos, nuestra preocupación por ellos y que experimenten nuestra preocupación por palabras y actos de amor…

Todos: Llena nuestros días de tu paz.

Guía: Que toda nuestra vida, aún en momentos de rutina y aburrimiento, se llene de un sentido de la presencia y providencia de Dios.

Todos: Llena nuestros días de tu paz.

Guía: Por aquellos que experimentan la vida como carga, los que sufren depresión, los abandonados, los enfermos…

Todos: Llena nuestros días de tu paz.

Guía: Por aquellos que han terminado el curso de su vida terrena y viven en la presencia eterna de Dios…

Todos: Llena nuestros días de tu paz.

Guía: *Pedimos si hay alguna otra interseción la digamos. Nosotros respondmas "Liena nuestros días de paz."*

Padre Nuestro

Guía: Unamos nuestras voces en las oraciones que primero aprendimos de aquellos que amamos y que son las que nutren el pan diario de nuestra oración:

Todos: *La asamblea reza el Padre Nuestro.*

Dios te Salve María

Guía: Compartimos la confianza de San Alfonso que María nos acompaña durante nuestras vidas y en la hora de la muerte; por tanto rezamos:

Todos: *La asamblea reza el Ave María.*

Bendición

Guía: Terminamos nuestra oración haciendo la señal de nuestra redención en Cristo sobre nosotros.

Todos: En el nombre del Padre, y del Hijo, y del Espíritu Santo. Amén.

RECOMENDACIONES PARA VIVIR
UNA VIDA CON DEVOCION

Coloca algo hermoso (una flor, un poco de fruta, una foto de alguien que quieres) cerca de tu cama donde lo puedes ver al despertar. Alaba a Dios por estos dones.

Cada mañana ház un trato con Dios que cada vez que haces cierta señal, como poner la mano sobre el corazón, estás manifestando por ello un acto de amor a Dios y un deseo de ver a Dios amado por todo el mundo.

Respira profundo e invita al Espíritu Santo, el aliento de Dios, a tu corazón.

Cuando oyes sonar el teléfono, ház una pausa para recordar la presencia de Dios en la persona que está llamando antes de que lo contestes.

Bebe un vaso de agua despacio y considera que desde toda la eternidad Dios estaba creando ese don de agua para reanimarte.

Pasa unos momentos varias veces hoy leyendo las sagradas escrituras, recordando, como dijo Alfonso, que no hay nada mejor para encender el amor de Dios en nosotros que la palabra de Dios que encontramos en las escrituras.

Escoge unas palabras de las escrituras y repítelas con frecuencia durante el día. Dice Alfonso, "Una frase sagrada, bien masticada, basta para hacernos santos."

Cuando te vistes, busca algo en tu armario que de veras no necesitas y regálaselo a alguien que sí lo necesita.

Alfonso y sus compañeros solían poner comida para los pobres al pie de una estatua del Niño Jesús durante cada comida. Abstente de una comida esta semana y envía el dinero a una organización que provee comida para niños pobres.

Toma un paseo y alaba a Dios por cada cosa hermosa que ves.

Compra o pide prestado la vida de un santo para leer y ház que esa persona sea tu compañero por la semana.

Recuerda que cada persona con quien te encuentras hoy es la verdadera morada de Dios. Ház un acto de comunión espiritual con la presencia de Jesús en ellos.

Ház una pausa en la mañana, al mediodía y en la tarde para poner la mano en tu corazón y recuerda la llegada de Dios en carne humana.

Piensa en Alfonso con su clavicordio mientras te deleitas en escuchar una pieza favorita de música.

Compra una vela especial que encenderás por unos momentos cada jueves en la tarde para recordar el gran don que Dios nos ha dado en la institución de la Eucaristía.

Los sábados dedica tiempo a obras de justicia y de paz en honor a María la Mujer de Misericordia.

True a la mente con frecuencia los misterios del amor de nuestro Salvador, cuando veas heno, un pesebre, una cueva, permite que esté presente en tu imaginación el Niño Jesús en el establo de Belén.

True a la mente con frecuencia los misterios del amor de nuestro Salvador, cuando veas un serrucho, un martillo, un cepillo, o una hacha, recuerda la vida de humilde labor que Ilevó nuestro Salvador en Nazaret.

True a la mente con frecuencia los misterios del amor de nuestro Salvador, cuando veas sogas, espinas, clavos y pedazos de madera, reflexiona sobre las Pasión y Muerte de nuestro Redentor.

True a la mente con frecuencia los misterios del amor de nuestro Salvador, cuando veas pan, uvas, vino o cualquier plato de comer, trae a la mente la grandeza del amor que Jesús nos tiene en darnos el Sacramento de la Eucaristía.

Todas las veces que puedas durante el día repite la oración, "Oh Dios, ven en mi auxilio. Señor, date prisa en socorrerme."

Todas las veces que puedas durante el día repite como oración, los nombres de Jesús y de María.

FREEDOM and TENDERNESS

CSSR

PART TWO

PRAYING THE REDEMPTORIST FEASTS

7

SAINT JOHN NEUMANN, PATHFINDER

Environment: In a prominent location place objects symbolic of Neumann's life and ministry: a picture of Neumann; map of Bohemia; flowers and plants (interest in botany); photograph or symbol of Philadelphia (city where he was bishop); symbols of the Eucharist (bread, wine, monstrance); crucifix (Neumann's episcopal motto, "Passion of Christ, strengthen me."); catechism (interest in religious education).

Opening Hymn

"You Satisfy the Hungry Heart": *Worship #736*
"O God, Our Help in Ages Past": *Worship #579*
"Seek Ye First the Kingdom of God": *Worship #580*
"All the Ends of the Earth": *Gather Comprehensive #520*
"Be Not Afraid": *Gather Comprehensive #608*
"On Eagle's Wings": *Gather Comprehensive #611*

Call to Prayer

Presider: John Neumann made his religious profession on January 16, 1842, at Saint James Parish in Baltimore, the first professed Redemptorist in North America. Writing in the house annals that day, a confrere punned, "In truth, a new man for our Congregation." In truth, the profession of John Neumann opened a new age for the Congregation—an age of growth and expansion; an age of energy and zeal; an age in which the dream of Alphonsus was carried to people and places he never imagined. We pray on this feast of John Neumann to be faithful to his example of imagination and zeal as we forge a path into the new age of the Congregation's life.

First Reading and Response

Reader 1: This is a reading from the Book of Revelation: 21:1–5.

Psalm Response

The presider divides the group into two choirs and each alternate saying one verse of the psalm.

Choir 1: Our great Lord
deserves great praise
in the city of God.

Choir 2: Holy mountain, beautiful height,
crown of the earth!
Zion, highest of sacred peaks,
city of the Great King!
God enthroned in its palaces
becomes our sure defense.

Choir 1: Watch the foreign kings
massing to attack;
seeing what they face,
they flee in terror.

Choir 2: Trembling grips them,
anguish like childbirth,
fury like an east wind
shattering a merchant fleet.

Choir 1: What we see matches what we were told,
"This is the city the Lord protects;
our God is strong forever."
In your temple, Lord,
we recall your constant love.

Choir 2: Your praise, like your name,
fills the whole world.
Your right hand holds the victory.
Mount Zion and the cities of Judah
rejoice at your justice.

Choir 1: March around Zion,
make the circuit, count each tower.
Ponder these walls,
observe these citadels.

Choir 2: So you may tell your children:
"Here is God! Our God forever!
God who leads us
even against death."

Choir 1: Glory be to God the Creator,
To Jesus the Christ,
And to the Spirit who dwells in our midst;
Now and forever. Amen.

Second Reading

Reader 2: This reading is from an account of the life of John Neumann taken from the writings of Blessed Francis X. Seelos, C.Ss.R.: "The years of 1845 and 1846 I spent in Pittsburgh where Father Neumann held to me the place of superior. I was his subject, no, rather his son. He was to me in every respect a father whom I can never forget. He taught me how to direct my steps in the practical ways of life. He cared for me in every way. The remembrance of his good example, his extreme modesty, his deep humility, his patience that over came all difficulties will ever be mine. He was accustomed to rise before the appointed hour and used to kindle the fire, bringing up the fuel himself, so that the room might be warm before I arose."

Pause for Silent Reflection

Third Reading

Reader 3: This reading is from a letter of Mother Caroline Friess, S.S.N.D., to John Berger, C.Ss.R.: "We were so happy to have had Father Neumann for several years as confessor and spiritual director and to get to know his holiness, scholarship, and kindness. He was a reliable teacher of the Catholic faith and a real friend of children. I often marveled at his calmness, gentleness, and perseverance in explaining religious concepts to children. In the year 1853 I complained to him about my assignment to be the superior of our Order in America—because of my youth, inexperience, and my incapacity. The holy man responded spontaneously and naturally, 'Sister, God strengthens and enlightens the young and the weak; submit yourself to humility. And, by the way, every superior makes mistakes. No person, no superior, exists who does not make mistakes or have doubts.' This consoled me and I felt satisfied to rely on the help of God."

Pause for Silent Reflection

Faith-Sharing

Presider: *The presider poses the following question and invites the group to spend some time sharing their responses with one another or with the group:*

What quality of John Neumann do we most need to forge a path into the future of the Redemptorists in this country?

Litany

Presider: For your dreams for the spread of the gospel in North America...
All: John, we remember you.
Presider: For your willingness to leave home and family for the sake of mission...
All: John, we remember you.
Presider: For your willingness to stretch yourself beyond your limitations and fears...
All: John, we remember you.
Presider: For your travels across the length and breadth of this new land...
All: John, we remember you.
Presider: For your love of your brothers in the Congregation...
All: John, we remember you.
Presider: For your dedication to education in faith that made a nation of immigrants into a vibrant church...
All: John, we remember you.
Presider: For your hours of letter writing, business dealings, your efforts to console and prod...
All: John, we remember you.
Presider: For the lifetime you gave to establishing religious life on our continent...
All: John, we remember you.
Presider: For your support of the ministry of women in the American Church...
All: John, we remember you.
Presider: For your struggles to learn different languages and to understand other cultures...
All: John, we remember you.

ST. JOHN NEUMANN PATHFINDER

Presider: For the heritage of imagination and risk-taking you left to the Redemptorists of the future…

All: John, we remember you.

Other phrases may be added, if desired.

The Our Father

Presider: John Neumann chose as his motto as bishop the words, "*Passio Christi conforta me*—Passion of Christ, be my strength." We sing together in the words of our Redeemer, who died and rose to new life; words that John Neumann prayed and taught others to pray:

All: *The assembly sings the Our Father.*

Closing Prayer

All: God of Bountiful Love, we rejoice today in our brother, John Neumann. Fill us with his zeal, his patience, his kindness. May we grow in faithfulness to the heritage that is ours. May we be new persons, filled with longing and energy for the new creation. We make our prayer in Jesus' name. Amen.

8

BLESSED PETER DONDERS: HEALER OF BODY AND SOUL

Environment: Create a tableau of a picture of Donders surrounded with candles and flowers; an attractive vessel of oil for anointing; and pictures and/or a map of Surinam.

Opening Song

"The Cry of the Poor": *Glory and Praise #61*

Opening Prayer

All: O Jesus our Redeemer, you took flesh and walked among us in search of the abandoned. Our brother, Peter Donders, spent his life in preaching your saving word to lepers, to slaves, to the poor and neglected. By his merits and prayers, stir up in us the same apostolic zeal, that we might place ourselves completely at the service of your gospel. You who live and reign with the Father and the Holy Spirit, One God, forever and ever. Amen.

Psalm Response

Presider: The presider organizes the assembly into two choirs who will alternately recite the parts of Psalm 42 that follow. The presider begins by praying the antiphon: "Jesus reached out his hand, touched the man, and said, 'Of course I want to heal you! Be clean!'"

Choir 1: Like the deer that yearns for running streams,
so my soul is yearning for you, my God.

Choir 2: My soul is thirsting for God, the living God.
When can I enter and see the face of God.

Choir 1: My tears have become my bread night and day,
and I hear it said all the day long: "Where is your God?"

Choir 2: I will remember these things as I pour out my soul: how I would lead the joyous procession into the house of God, with cries of gladness and thanksgiving, the multitude wild with joy.

Choir 1: Why are you so sad, my soul? Why sigh within me? Hope in God; for I will yet praise my savior and my God.

Choir 2: My soul is downcast within me when I think of you, from the land of Jordan and Mount Hermon, from the hill of Mizar.

Choir 1: Deep is calling on deep as the waterfalls roar; your breakers and all your waves crashed over me.

Choir 2: By day Yahweh will send loving kindness; by night I will sing praise to the God of my life.

Choir 1: I will say to God my rock: "Why have you forgotten me? Why do I go mourning, oppressed by the foe?"

Choir 2: With cries that pierce me to the heart, my enemies revile me, saying to me all day: "Where is your God?"

Choir 1: Why are you oppressed, my soul—why cry within me? Hope in God; I will praise Yahweh, my savior and my God.

Choir 2: Glory to you, Source of all Being, Eternal Word, and Holy Spirit.

Choir 1: As it was in the beginning, is now, and will be forever. Amen.

All: Jesus reached out his hand, touched the man, and said, "Of course I want to heal you! Be clean"

Readings and Responses

Reader 1: Peter Donders, though already a priest, chose to become a Redemptorist, drawn by the desire to live and work in community. He wrote, "From the day on which, by God's grace, I was received into the Congregation, I do not think I ever passed a day, or even an hour, without experiencing great joy in my holy vocation and in community, except for the odd trial or temptation which I got over, by God's grace."

All: One thing I ask of Yahweh: This I seek—to dwell in your house all the days of my life (Psalm 27).

Reader 2: Donders knew the discouragement that comes from hard work with meager results. He writes, "I have been working here for more than twenty years and what meager results I have gained! If I were not convinced that God can do all things and that, in his infinite mercy, he can enlighten minds and change hearts, I would loose courage."

All: Trust in Yahweh and do good so that you will dwell in the land and enjoy security. Take delight in Yahweh and you will receive the desire of your heart (Psalm 37).

Reader 3: Bishop Schaap, a Redemptorist and Donders's ordinary, wrote of him: "As a son of Saint Alphonsus he had all the genial playfulness that distinguished his holy Father. He can never tell me enough how greatly edified he is to see the spirit of holy joy reign among us. How delightful it is to see Father Donders lighting up his pipe and puffing away at recreation."

All: How good it is, how pleasant, for God's people to live in unity (Psalm 133).

Reader 4: With the voice of a prophet, Peter Donders spoke against the slave trade: "Woe! Woe! to thee, Surinam, on the great day of accounting. Yes, woe! Woe, a thousand times to those Europeans—planters, slave holders, managers, overseers, and officials to whom this slave population is subject! Woe to those who make fortunes out of the sweat and blood of those unfortunate creatures who have God alone to defend them!"

All: *(From Psalm 72)*
They shall rescue the poor when they cry out
And the afflicted who have no one to help them.
They shall save the lives of the poor.
From oppression and violence they shall redeem them
And precious shall their blood be.

Reader 5: Our Constitutions (Statute 05) say that Blessed Peter Donders was "distinguished for his missionary service dedicated to the whole human person." Donders did not merely preach. He dressed the sores of lepers with his own hands. He said that a school was just as important for a mission as a chapel. When he died some of his people asked, "Now who will teach us to sing?"

All: *(From Psalm 23)*
Yahweh, you are my shepherd.
I shall not want.
You shall spread the table before me
in the sight of my foes.
You anoint my head with oil.
My cup overflows.

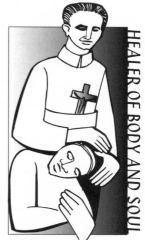

BLESSED PETER DONDERS

HEALER OF BODY AND SOUL

Reader 6: This is a reading from the Gospel of Luke: 6:17–26.

Silent Meditation

Presider: You are now invited to silently meditate on the readings we have just heard.

Concluding Prayer

Presider: We conclude our prayer by reciting the ancient Christian hymn of praise, the "*Te Deum*," which was prayed daily by Peter Donders. We acclaim the God whose holiness is made manifest in Peter Donders. We thank the God who gave Peter Donders to our Congregation. We pray God to make us worthy to be in the company of the saints with Peter, our brother. *The presider indicates that each verse of the "Te Deum" is to be recited by a different member of the assembly, each in turn.*

Speaker 1: We long for you O God, we confess our deep desire;
for the heavens are arrayed with your unhidden beauty,
and the entire earth surrenders to your touch.

Speaker 2: The powers of everlasting light cry aloud to you;
the holy and ancient places of darkness continually cry your name.

Speaker 3: Saints in every generation speak your outrageous glory;
those who have seen and proclaimed you are passionate with praise;
those who have cried for justice are satisfied in you;
those who carried you in their wounds are bodied forth with life.
Your holy and stumbling church throughout all the world
is filled with your desire.

Speaker 4: Merciful creator, of infinite tenderness;
wounded Redeemer, by whom all flesh is moved,
comforter of fire, who lead us into truth;
God, difficult and beautiful, we offer you our praise.

Speaker 5: You are the source of our yearning, O Christ;
you are the way of glory.
Bearing our sweet and humble flesh, fruit of a woman's womb,
you were made and molded as we are
by particular human touch.

Speaker 6: Breaking forth from the tomb you opened wide our hearts, turning the sharpness of death to the terror of new life and of desire fulfilled.

Speaker 7: We believe that you will come, our lover and our judge: increase our longing for justice in your afflicted world, that we may be counted among your saints in glory, and know ourselves beloved.

Speaker 8: Spirit of discernment, integrity, and fire; breathe on our fearfulness, refine our truthfulness, and speak through our speechlessness; that we may daily refuse what is evil, and be taken up with praise.

This version of the "Te Deum" is from Janet Morley, All Desires Known—Inclusive Prayers for Worship and Meditation *(Harrisburg, PA: Morehouse Publishing, 1992), 33–4.*

Blessing

The members of the assembly approach the presider who anoints the head of each with oil as he says to them, "Be whole."

Closing Antiphon

Standing before the altar, the assembly concludes the prayer service by singing the "Salve Regina."

Salve Regina, mater misericordiae:
Vita, dulcedo et spes nostra salve.
Ad te clamamus, exsules filii Hevae.
Ad te suspiramus, gementes et flentes
in hac lacrimarum valle. Eia ergo,
advocata nostra, illos tuos miseri-
cordes oculos ad nos converte.
Et jesum benedictum fructum ventris
tui, nobis post hoc ex silium o-
stende. O clemens, O pia,
O dulcis Virgo Maria.

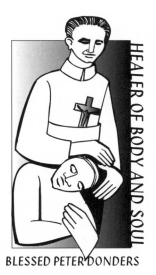

HEALER OF BODY AND SOUL

BLESSED PETER DONDERS

9

SAINT CLEMENT HOFBAUER: TO SATISFY THE HEART

Environment: Symbols of Clement's life and ministry may be placed at a focal point in the room: Bible, C.Ss.R. mission cross, book of the Visits (reading these drew Clement to the Redemptorists), loaf of bread (symbol of Clement's career as baker and also of the Eucharist), purple stole (symbol of Clement as confessor), olive branch (title of a Catholic journal founded on Clement's initiative), flags or other symbols of Poland and Austria.

Introduction

Presider: Praise and thanks to God who gave Clement Hofbauer to the Church to preach the Gospel anew for a new age.

All: Praise and thanks to God for our brother Clement.

Opening Song

"For All the Saints": *Worship #705*
"By All Your Saints Still Striving": *Worship #706*
"Ye Watchers and Ye Holy Ones": *Worship #707*

First Reading and Response

Reader 1: A reading from *Saint Clement Maria Hofbauer* by John Hofer, C.Ss.R.: "Clement, reflecting on religious conditions in Northern Europe, said, 'Since I have had the opportunity as papal legate to compare the conditions of Catholics in Poland with those of Protestants in Germany, I have become convinced that the great falling away of the Church in Germany took place because the people stood, as they now stand, in need of the uplifting power of religion. The Reformation was brought about and maintained not so much by heretics and philosophers, as by the great body of people earnestly seeking a religion that would satisfy the heart. I have told this to the Pope and to the Cardinals in Rome but they would not believe me.'"

Presider: We pray for the people of our time who long for a religion that will satisfy the heart.

All: May all people find in the Church a community of light, welcome, and warmth.

Presider: We pray for poets, musicians, artists, and those who work in the media.

All: May they use their gifts to draw people to the goodness and beauty of God.

Presider: Clement was the first to associate oblates to the mission of the Congregation.

All: May his spirit lead us to discern new ways of collaborating with the laity as equal partners in ministry.

Presider: Clement loved to pour over maps of North America and dreamed of establishing the Congregation on this continent.

All: We are the fulfillment of Clement's dream. May we grow more deeply in love with the Congregation and our mission.

Presider: Clement loved the liturgy of the Church and took great care to celebrate the sacred mysteries with devotion and splendor.

All: May we grow in reverence for the mysteries we celebrate and proclaim.

Presider: All the foundations established by Clement were also centers of works for justice and peace—schools, orphanages, printing presses, and shelters for the poor.

All: May our ministries attend to the needs of the whole human person, created and loved by God.

Presider: We invite members of the group to add any additional spontaneous petitions that they may wish.

Second Reading and Response

Reader 2: A contemporary of Clement made this reflection on his preaching: "The marvelous attractive power of his sermons must be traced to no other source than his strong, living faith—a faith that had become, as it were, the very breath of his life and an essential part of his very being. To give one simple example: when preaching on the Incarnation, Clement would reverently clasp his hands as he said, 'Our very own flesh he has taken unto himself!' These simple words uttered with an apostle's conviction impressed all his hearers. Clement put into practice in his life and preaching the words with which John begins one of his letters, 'That which we have heard, which we have seen with our own eyes, which we have looked upon, and our hearts have touched, we declare to you.'"

All: What was from the beginning, what we have heard,
    what we have seen with our own eyes, what we have looked upon
    and touched with our own hands
    is the Word of Life.
    For this life was made visible
    and we have seen it and give witness to it.
    This Eternal Life was with the Father
    and was made visible to us.
    What we have seen and heard we now proclaim
    so that we may be in communion with one another.
    Our communion is with the Father,
    and with his Son, Jesus the Christ.

Faith-Sharing

The following may be used for faith-sharing:

Presider: Gerard Arbuckle gives the following characteristics of refounding persons in religious communities: closeness to people; creative imagination and listening; commitment to hard work; commitment to small beginnings; toleration of failure; an orientation to community; a capacity to see the paschal mystery in rejection and suffering. How does the life and example of Saint Clement, which remarkably exemplifies these qualities, inspire our efforts toward the refounding of Redemptorist life today? I invite members of the assembly to share with one another or with the group their thoughts on this question.

Closing

Presider: The psychologist Rollo May wrote that "only the truth that is experienced at all levels of being has the power to change the human person." Clement was a man who experienced the Gospel in the very depths of himself and so his preaching and his ministry were able to change hearts and transform lives. We pray that those transforming truths of Clement's may be ours.

The presider leads the members of the assembly in the following response:

Presider: Clement broke the bread of the Eucharist to satisfy the hungry hearts.
All: May we experience the truth of Eucharist in our entire being.

Presider: A contemporary of Clement said, "The rich go looking for Clement but Clement is off looking for the poor."

All: May we experience the truth of our Call to the Poor in our entire being.

Presider: Clement had a genius for friendship and he said that his life was never the same again after the death of his close friend and confrere Thaddeus Hubl.

All: May we experience the truth of Gospel Friendship in our entire being.

Presider: Clement called the rosary "my library."

All: May we experience the truth of the Perpetual Help of Mary in our entire being.

Presider: Clement was above all else a man of the Church.

All: May we experience the truth of Faith in our entire being.

Closing

Presider: As we close our time of prayer together, we listen to the words of encouragement that Clement directed to his confreres of Saint Benno's in 1806 and which he directs to us, his confreres of today: "Courage! God is in charge. He directs all to his glory and our good and nothing can resist God. My dear brothers, let us keep ourselves from sin and strive for holiness. Let us encourage and inspire each other to do good. Practice charity among yourselves. I greet you all in the heart of Jesus."

Sign of Peace

Presider: Let us offer a sign of peace to one another saying, "I greet you in the heart of Jesus."

Closing Antiphon

Presider: Let us close this prayer service by singing the "*Salve Regina.*" The words may be found on page 57.

10

JOSEPH: MAN OF DREAMS, MAN OF JUSTICE

Environment: A picture or statue of Saint Joseph; tools; pictures of families; and a Bible are placed in a spot visible to the assembly.

Opening Song

"Sing With All the Saints in Glory": *Gather Comprehensive* #442

Opening Prayer

Presider: Blessed be the Lord the God of Israel.

All: He has come to his people and set them free.

Presider: Let us pray together words of a song written by Saint Alphonsus as a lullaby to be sung by Joseph to the child Jesus.

All: Since you the name of father have bestowed
On me, my Jesus, let me call you Son.
My Son! I love—I love you; yes, my God,
Forever will I love you, dearest one!

Since you are pleased to share my humble home
And be on earth companion of my love.
Well may I hope, dear Jesus, to become
Your loved companion in your home above.

Reading and Response

Reader 1: This is a reading from the Gospel of Matthew: 1:18–25.

Presider: The liturgy sees in Joseph the man of justice of whom the psalms speak. We pray together in the words of the psalm; words of prayer that Jesus would have learned from the lips of Joseph.

All: Oh, how great is the joy of those
who do not follow the advice of the wicked,
nor follow the sinner's path,
nor sit in company with the cynical.
Rather, they delight in the law of Yahweh,
they meditate on it night and day.
They are like the tree
planted near streams of water,
that yields its fruit in due season.
Just as its leaves never wither,
so all that they do prospers.
The wicked are not like this.
They are like chaff driven about by the wind.
Therefore, the wicked cannot survive judgment,
nor will they stand in the assembly of the just.
God watches over the way of the just,
but the way of the wicked leads to doom.

Glory to you, Source of All Being,
Eternal Word, and Holy Spirit.
As it was in the beginning, is now,
and will be forever. Amen.

Ritual

Presider: In the synagogue service, the rabbi passes through the congregation with the scroll of the Torah. The people touch the scroll and kiss their fingers as a sign of reverence for the Word of God. I invite you now to do the same, conscious that this gesture of reverence was performed in the same way by Jesus and Joseph. *The presider then walks through the assembly with the Bible which all reverence as indicated.*

Faith-Sharing

Presider: I invite members of the assembly, if they so desire, to share their experience of faith in response to one of the following questions:

1. Share an experience of someone you know who is a good father and describe the qualities that make him so, conscious that this was the role that Joseph played in the life of Jesus.
2. Joseph is the patron of workers and reminds us that work is a noble participation in the creative will of God. Have you ever had an experience of work that was also an experience of the holy?

Litany of Saint Joseph

Presider: The presider invites the assembly to say the Litany of Saint Joseph. The presider prays the invocations and the assembly makes the response in unison, or the invocations may be said by different members of the group in turn with the assembly praying the response.

P. Holy Trinity, one God	A. *Have mercy on us.*
P. Holy Mary, wife of Joseph	A. *Pray for us.*
P. Saint Joseph	A. *Pray for us.*
P. Husband of Mary	A. *Pray for us.*
P. Teacher of Jesus	A. *Pray for us.*
P. Son of David	A. *Pray for us.*
P. Man of justice	A. *Pray for us.*
P. Man of vision	A. *Pray for us.*
P. Man of courage	A. *Pray for us.*
P. Man of silence	A. *Pray for us.*
P. Patron of the contemplative life	A. *Pray for us.*
P. Model of fathers	A. *Pray for us.*
P. Comforter of the dying	A. *Pray for us.*
P. That we may see God present in our daily labors	A. *Saint Joseph, pray for us.*
P. That love and forgiveness may flourish in families	A. *Saint Joseph, pray for us.*
P. That we all see sexuality as God's gift	A. *Saint Joseph, pray for us.*
P. For a respect for human life, especially of the weak and helpless	A. *Saint Joseph, pray for us.*
P. That all the members of the Church will grow in holiness	A. *Saint Joseph, pray for us.*

P. That healing and peace may come to those who are
victims of violence and abuse in their homes   A. *Saint Joseph, pray for us.*

P. That the dying may experience the comfort
of God's presence   A. *Saint Joseph, pray for us.*

All may now add their own petitions to which the assembly responds, "Saint Joseph, pray for us."

Closing Prayer

Presider: Let us pray. God, creator and sustainer of the universe, in every age you call men and women to develop their gifts for the good of others. With Saint Joseph as our example and guide, help us to do the work you have asked of us and come to the rewards you have promised. We ask this through our Lord, Jesus Christ, your Son, who lives and reigns with you and the Holy Spirit, one God, forever and ever.

All: Amen.

Blessing

Presider: The presider invites each to place his hand on the shoulder of the person next to him or her as the presider says the ancient Hebrew blessing:

May the Lord bless us and keep us.
May the Lord make his face to shine upon us.
May the Lord look upon us kindly and
    give us peace,
now and forever.

All: Amen.

Joseph

Man of Dreams, Man of Justice

MARY, PERPETUAL HELP OF GOD'S PEOPLE

Environment: The icon of Our Lady of Perpetual Help surrounded by flowers and candles is placed in a central location.

Opening Hymn

The traditional "O Mother of Perpetual Help" hymn or other suitable Marian song is sung.

Introduction

Presider: May our God, close to humanity and ever ready to help us, be with you.
All: And also with you.

Call to Prayer

Presider: From the beginning, our Congregation has experienced the intercession of Mary, the Mother of God, and has been marked by a special devotion to her. We have preached her glories and confided in her prayers. In 1866, Pope Pius IX gave the icon of Our Lady of Perpetual Help to us and our devotion to Mary was given its characteristic face. As we begin our prayer, let us listen to the song of Saint Alphonsus, "*O Bella Mia Speranza*," and gaze on the image of Our Mother of Perpetual Help. What memories arise in us as we rest in the compassionate gaze of Mary, our perpetual help?

A recording of the Alphonsian hymn "O Bella Mia Speranza" is played during a period of silent prayer.

Readings and Responses

Reader 1: This is a reading from the Book of Revelation: 12:1–10a.

All: *(from Revelation 10–12a)*

> Now have salvation and power come,
> the reign of our God and the authority of God's Anointed.
> The great accuser is cast out,
> who accuses humanity night and day before our God.
> They conquered him by the blood of the Lamb
> and by the word of their testimony.
> Love for life did not deter them from death.
> Rejoice, you heavens,
> Rejoice you who dwell in them!

Presider: Our Lady of Perpetual Help has been a great sign of God's desire to redeem and liberate. Through Mary, God continues to act in history to defeat every power that oppresses and to foster new life. In the traditional novena to Our Mother of Perpetual Help, people wrote thanksgivings for the favors they had received through Mary's intercession. These were read aloud to give voice to their experience of the power of God and Mary's intercession. Let us listen to the testimonies of those who have known God's care through Our Lady of Perpetual Help.

Reader 2: From a letter of Charles de Foucauld, Little Brother of Jesus, November 8, 1896: "We arrived in Rome at 1:30 on Friday afternoon....First we went to Saint Mary Major and then to the church of Saint Alphonsus where there is a picture of Our Lady of Perpetual Help, a title that suits the blessed Virgin so well! We need her perpetual help so much, we who are so weak and stumbling! For a long time now, and particularly for the last three years, I have been under her special protection. This is how it happened: three years ago I had many difficulties regarding my interior life—fears, anxieties, periods of darkness: I wanted to serve God, I was afraid of offending him, I couldn't see things straight, I suffered; so I placed myself with all my heart under the protection of Our Lady of Perpetual Help. I implored her to guide my footsteps as she had guided those of the Infant Jesus, and to lead me in all things in such a way as not to offend God, but rather to be a subject of consolation for our Lord Jesus Christ; in such a way as to console as much as I could the heart of Jesus that sees and loves us. So it was very sweet for me to stand beneath the picture of our so dear and good Mother on my very first day, in my very first hour. Need I say that I commended you to her from all that is best in my heart, and I said for you as much as for myself, 'Our Lady of Perpetual Help, grant me your all powerful help and the grace always to ask for it.'"

Reader 3: This reading is by Sister M. Rosario Battung, a Filipina Sister of the Good Shepherd: "Tens of thousands flock to Baclaran Church every Wednesday. From dawn to dawn, rain or shine, people from all walks of life flock to this National Shrine of Our Lady of Perpetual Help, confident that Mary, the compassionate Mother of Jesus their God will listen and help them in their need....The devotees of Our Lady of Perpetual Help pray in a very special manner. Very remarkable is the concentrated prayer/contemplation experienced by all who come to her shrine. It is amazing how silent thousands of people can be, intensely praying not only for themselves but for the others present in the shrine or elsewhere, for their needs and intentions....Starting with their existential experience of pain and grief, joy and success, a critical need or a crisis situation in their lives, all who approach or write to Mary as a woman of compassion, are certain that she will enter fully into their situation....Truly, as in Hosea, God comes to us, as certain as the coming of the dawn or the rain of early spring."

Faith-Sharing

Presider: Members of the assembly are now invited to share with a neighbor or with the whole group an experience in their lives of the action of God through Our Mother of Perpetual Help.

Pause for Sharing

Intercessions

Presider: Mother of Perpetual Help, your image is bathed in golden light.

All: Help us to recognize that our lives and our world are permeated by God's presence.

Presider: Mother of Perpetual Help, Jesus, frightened by the prospect of his future torture and death, fled to your arms for shelter.

All: Help us to make our Church and our Congregation places where the frightened little ones of our world may find welcome and comfort.

Presider: Mother of Perpetual Help, your hands cradled the Word-made-flesh.

All: Help us to spend ourselves in the service of the coming of the reign of Jesus.

Presider: Mother of Perpetual Help, your gaze looks beyond us into the future glory of God's reign.

All: Help us to be a voice of hope and builders of the future.

Presider: Mother of Perpetual Help, your icon shines with the colors of the spectrum, a rainbow of peace between heaven and earth.

All: Help us to be bridges of reconciliation among peoples and between humans and God.

Presider: Spontaneous petitions are offered to Our Lady of Perpetual Help.

Closing Prayer

Presider: We join our voices with the voice of Mary in her song of praise. *A musical setting of the* Magnificat *may be sung or the following may be recited.*

My soul proclaims the greatness of the Lord;
my spirit rejoices in God my Savior.
For he has looked upon his handmaid's lowliness;
behold, all ages to come will call me blessed.
The Mighty One has done great things for me,
Holy is God's name.
God's mercy is from age to age
to those who fear him.
He has shown might with his arm,
dispersed the arrogant of mind and heart.
He has thrown down rulers from their thrones
but lifted up the lowly.
The hungry God has filled with good things:
the rich he has sent away empty.
God has remembered his servant Israel,
ever mindful of his mercy,
according the promise made to our ancestors,
to Abraham and Sarah and their descendants forever. Amen.

PERPETUAL HELP OF GOD'S PEOPLE

MARY

Blessing

Presider: *The presider says the traditional words of blessing:*

Through the prayers of our holy father Saint Alphonsus and the intercession of Our Mother of Perpetual Help, may the blessing of almighty God, the Father, the Son, and the Holy Spirit, come upon you and remain forever.

All: Amen.

Closing Antiphon

Presider: The assembly is invited to close this prayer service by singing the *"Salve Regina."* The words to this antiphon may be on page 57.

BLESSED GENNARO SARNELLI: TEACHER OF PRAYER, PROPHET OF JUSTICE

Environment: All gather in a circle to pray. In the center of the circle is a lighted candle and other symbols of Sarnelli's life and ministry, for example, a Redemptorist mission cross; a picture of Sarnelli; a photograph of a local "red light" district; photographs of people gathered to pray or of Christian communities.

Opening Song

"We Are Called": *Gather Comprehensive* #718
"Voices That Challenge": *Gather Comprehensive* #721
"We Shall Overcome": *Gather Comprehensive* #742

Opening Prayer

Presider: May the God of Gennaro Sarnelli, the God who welcomes the outcast,
    be with you.
All: May the God of compassion live in our hearts forever.

Presider: Let us pray.
All: Jesus, beloved companion, you share our table and our lives. We know that we are sinners. We know as well, that, at a deeper level, we have been chosen, redeemed, and gathered together in your name. Make our church a place of welcome and our hearts as wide as your mercy. Amen.

Readings and Responses

Presider: Our brother Gennaro was a teacher of prayer. One of his books is entitled, *The World Sanctified by the Practice of Mental Prayer Made in Common*. He shared the Redeemer's own confidence that where two or three are gathered in God's name the earth become holy ground. Let us listen to the word of God and to the words of our brother Gennaro and become present to the Redeemer dwelling among us gathered here.

Reader 1: This is a reading from the Gospel according to Matthew: 9:10–12.

Pause for Silent Meditation

Reader 2: This is a reading from a letter of Sarnelli to Saint Alphonsus: "I have a special favor to ask you. Every time you say Mass, as you break the host and place the small fragment in the chalice, place there my heart too and ask Jesus that he will give me the zeal and strength necessary for my vocation."

Pauses for Silent Meditation

Reader 3: Cast yourself into the immense womb of God. Widen your heart and trust without limit. Say with Saint Paul, "I can do all things in God who gives me strength."

Pause for Silent Meditation

Reader 4: Prayer can find gold amidst mud and draw water from the rocks.

There is now a longer pause of several minutes. At the end of the period of silent prayer, the presider invites each person to share his or her prayer by speaking one word aloud that summarizes how God has spoken to them today. At the conclusion of the sharing, the presider says:

Presider: Our brother Gennaro was a prophet of justice. Listen to these words from one of his conferences:

Reader 5: "How many wealthy live today in Christendom! They spend their time at banquets, at feastings and diversions while the poor of Jesus Christ die of hunger. How many servants and hired hands are defrauded of their just recompense. How the poor struggle to collect what they have earned and would to God that they got it intact! How many rich there are that have a superabundance of everything—except of God. The rich do not wish to give the Lord in the person of the poor even a fraction of the goods of this world—not even to gain eternal life. The strictest judgment is reserved for those who have acted without mercy toward their neighbor."

Closing Prayer

Presider: Let us bring to prayer the needs of those so dear to Sarnelli, the poor, the abused, the victimized.

The presider invites the group to offer names of groups of people who are oppressed or victimized; the group responds with "Bring them healing, Spirit of Life." The presider begins with the following three groups.

Presider: For prostitutes…
All: Bring them healing, Spirit of Life.
Presider: For runaway children…
All: Bring them healing, Spirit of Life.
Presider: For those who cannot pray…
All: Bring them healing, Spirit of Life.

The Our Father

Presider: United with Gennaro Sarnelli, we pray as Jesus taught us.

The assembly joins in singing the Our Father.

Blessing

The presider takes the candle from the center of the circle and it is passed from one person to the next as each says to the person next to him or her these words frequently used by Sarnelli as a blessing: "May Jesus Christ be our light!"

TEACHER OF PRAYER PROPHET OF JUSTICE

BLESSED GENNARO SARNELLI

FEAST OF THE MOST HOLY REDEEMER: THIRD SUNDAY IN JULY

Environment: In a central location is placed the paschal candle, a C.Ss.R. mission cross, and a Bible opened to Isaiah 61.

Opening Song

"Hail Redeemer, King Divine"
"Lift High the Cross": *Worship* #704
"To Jesus Christ, Our Sovereign King": *Worship* #497

Invitation to Prayer

Presider: We begin our prayer by marking ourselves with the cross, the sign of our Redemption. In the Name of the Father, and of the Son, and of the Holy Spirit. Amen. May the fullness of life and peace of Jesus the Redeemer be with you all.

All: And also with you.

Reading and Response

Presider: Let us listen to the words of the prophet Isaiah. In listening to these words, Jesus the Redeemer, discovered his own vocation. In praying this text, Alphonsus found his own vision for the Redemptorist Congregation. To make this prophetic dream a reality is the reason the Congregation of the Most Holy Redeemer exists in the world.

Reader: This is a reading from the prophet Isaiah: Chapter 61:1–11.

Presider: We respond to the word of God, in the words of our Constitutions:

The presider asks individual members of the assembly to read each of the following responses. Alternately, they may be read by members of the assembly, either one after another, or spontaneously.

1. The Spirit of the Lord is upon us to make us "humble and courageous servants among people of the Gospel of Christ the Redeemer who is head and model of the new humanity" (Chapter 1, Article 1, Paragraph 6).

2. The Spirit of the Lord is upon us to "proclaim before everything else the very high destiny of the individual and of the whole human race (Chapter 1, Article 2, Paragraph 7).

3. The Spirit of the Lord is upon us to "raise up and develop communities that will walk worthily in the vocation to which they are called, and exercise the priestly, prophetic, and royal offices with which God has endowed them (Chapter 1, Article 3, Paragraph 12).

4. The Spirit of the Lord is upon us to "carry out [our] mission with bold initiative and whole hearted dedication" (Chapter 1, Article 4, Paragraph 13).

5. The Spirit of the Lord is upon us preventing us from settling down "in surroundings and structures in which [our] work would be no longer missionary" (Chapter 1, Article 4, Paragraph 15).

6. The Spirit of the Lord is upon us to "diligently pioneer new ways of preaching the Gospel to every creature" (Chapter 1, Article 4, Paragraph 15).

7. The Spirit of the Lord is upon us to reveal the "all embracing nature of redemption and give witness to the truth that whoever follows Christ, the perfect human being, becomes more human" (Chapter 1, Article 6, Paragraph 19).

8. The Spirit of the Lord is upon us to live in a spirit of "genuinely brotherly union, to combine [our] prayers, [our] labors, [our] successes and failures, and [our] material goods, for the service of the Gospel (Chapter 2, Article 1, Paragraph 22).

9. The Spirit of the Lord is upon us to enable us to "see God in the people and in the events of everyday life and to be able to distinguish between what is real and what is illusory (Chapter 2, Article 2, Paragraph 24).

10. The Spirit of the Lord is upon us so that we, like Mary, "may walk [our] pilgrim way in faith and embrace with [our] whole heart the saving will of God (Chapter 2, Article 3, Paragraph 32).

Faith-Sharing

Presider: *The presider asks the assembly to respond to the following question.*

Where do you see the vision of Isaiah 61 coming to fulfillment in the world today? Where in the Congregation?

Ritual

Presider: Let us express our gratitude for the gift of the Redemption and of our Redemptorist vocation by venerating the cross, sign of love's triumph over sin and death.

The C.Ss.R. mission cross is passed through the assembly and each person venerates it by a kiss or other sign of veneration.

Renewal of Vows

The presider invites all to come forward and to place their hands together on the Bible open to Isaiah.

Presider: Let us recommit ourselves to the vision of Isaiah 61 and to each other as we renew our religious profession. The response to each part of the renewal is "The Spirit of the Lord is upon me!"

Presider: Christ emptied himself, taking the form of a servant. Do you wish like him to dedicate your entire life to the work of the Redemption?

All: The Spirit of the Lord is upon me!

Presider: Do you wish to dedicate yourself totally to the mission of Christ and share his self-renunciation, the virginal freedom of his heart, and his wholehearted offering of himself for the life of the world?

All: The Spirit of the Lord is upon me!

Presider: Do you wish to live your union with God in the form of apostolic charity and, through missionary charity, seek God's glory?

All: The Spirit of the Lord is upon me!

Closing Antiphon

Presider: We ask the prayers of Mary to obtain for us perseverance in the mission of the Redeemer as we sing together the "*Salve Regina.*" The words to this antiphon are on page 57.

Blessing

Presider: We conclude our prayer by offering one another a sign of peace.

OUR FATHER THROUGH OTHERS' EYES: PRAYER FOR THE FEAST OF SAINT ALPHONSUS LIGUORI

Environment: In a central location is placed an image of Saint Alphonsus surrounded with flowers and candles and a basket containing the questions that will be distributed. These questions, listed in the box at the end of this prayer service, should be copied on individual pieces of paper, enough for all those present.

Opening Song

"There's a Wideness in God's Mercy": *Worship* #595
"Lord, Whose Love in Humble Service": *Worship* #630
"You Have Anointed Me": *Gather Comprehensive* #676
"God Has Chosen Me": *Gather Comprehensive* #682

Call to Prayer

Presider: May the God of Loveliness,
        may Jesus the Redeemer of the oppressed,
        may the Spirit of holy freedom,
        may the God of Alphonsus Liguori, be with you!
All: And also with you!

Readings and Responses

Presider: Alphonsus Liguori—he watches us from stained-glass windows and portraits and statues. We used to put his initials at the head of all our papers along with those of Jesus, Mary, and Joseph. His books line our library shelves, dozens of red or green volumes: We call him founder. We call him father. Like any father, the thought of him comforts and nourishes us. He challenges us and sometimes embarrasses us and makes us feel guilty. Sometimes he feels more like a great-great-grandfather than a father; a distant patriarch, the head of the clan, whom we revere but can't say we feel close to or know. As we celebrate his memory in prayer today, we will listen to the voices of others telling us how they saw our father. We will look at our father through others' eyes. May their testimony engender pride in us that we are sons of Alphonsus Liguori. May we feel his blood coursing through our veins and his spirit enlivening ours.

Between each of the following readings is sung this refrain: "All the ends of the earth have seen the power of God; All the ends of the earth have seen the power of God. (See Gather Comprehensive *#95.)*

Reader 1: Father Bruno Lanteri of Turin, founder of the Oblates of the Blessed Virgin Mary, was only twenty-eight years old when Alphonsus died but even then he had a devotion to the person and writings of the servant of God. He used to relate an anecdote that made a great impression on him. A few days after the news of the holy founder's death, Lanteri was walking through the streets of Turin when he heard himself being called several times. Turning around he saw a woman, a poor fruit seller, who asked him sadly, "Is it true that Bishop Liguori is dead?" "It is quite true," he answered. "Then," said the woman, giving him a stipend, "would you say a Mass for the repose of his soul? If you only knew all that I owe him! I had long been afflicted with troubles of mind so terrible and continual that they never left me a moment's rest; but one of his little Books fell into my hands and ever since my peace of mind has been restored."

All: *The assembly sings this refrain:* All the ends of the earth have seen the power of God; All the ends of the earth have seen the power of God.

Reader 2: The following is a reading from "A Journey With Alphonsus," by Sister Anne Munley, I.H.M.: "The spirituality and the example of Alphonsus have much to offer to the hurting world of today. Alphonsus was an extraordinarily gifted, insightful, and compassionate person. He had a fine mind and a heart made large by loving. All that he was and all that he did flowed from his own deep and intimate experience of a caring and approachable God of love and loveliness. His whole being was focused on proclaiming the lavishness of God's love and on uniting his love for Jesus the Redeemer with love for the poor....He had an exquisite sensitivity to the love of God active and alive in the hearts of the poor and neglected and was a persistent voice for them. He saw that existing church structures and spirituality were not touching them and with considerable creativity and imagination he developed new ways to reach out and evangelize….His recognition that deep friendship with God is possible for ordinary people is a prophetic message that is much needed in these times. May we, in creative fidelity to his spirit, proclaim with our lives the loving and accessible God of Alphonsus."

All: *The assembly sings the following refrain:* All the ends of the earth have seen the power of God; All the ends of the earth have seen the power of God.

Reader 3: On September 21, 1996, almost two thousand people, Redemptorists and their friends, gathered in Washington, D.C., to share Eucharist and a meal and to tell the story of Alphonsus Liguori. We watched Roberta Nobleman, an Englishwoman, a Protestant, tell the story of Alphonsus from the perspective of Mary, the peasant girl of Nazareth. At the conclusion of the play, Nobleman said, "Wherever Alphonsus is, there is light and warmth and color!"

The next day the charismatic prayer group of Immaculate Conception in the Bronx met and a woman shared this reflection of her experience of the celebration the day before: "The dinner yesterday was like an image of heaven for me—all different kinds of people, rich and poor, priests and lay people, of many different cultures and races, all seated at table with one another, sharing a meal and telling stories."

All: *The assembly sings the following refrain:* All the ends of the earth have seen the power of God; All the ends of the earth have seen the power of God.

Faith-Sharing

Presider: *The presider invites the group to a period of faith-sharing in response to the following questions:*

When you hear these stories people have told about Alphonsus, what stirs in you? Do you have a story that has given you a new appreciation of Alphonsus?

Prayer

Presider: Alphonsus was very reticent about himself and his own personal experience. He never wrote an autobiography or a spiritual journal. His remarks about his own life experience are very few. There was only one story he wanted told about himself. There was one text in which he saw his life mirrored. It is the Gospel passage from Luke 4. Let us pray this passage together. Let us see our Father Alphonsus through the eyes of Jesus the Redeemer:

All: The Spirit of the Lord is upon me,
because he has anointed me
to bring glad tidings to the poor.
He has sent me
to proclaim liberty to captives,
recovery of sight to the blind,
to let the oppressed go free,
and to proclaim a year acceptable
to the Lord.

Solemnity of
SAINT ALPHONSUS LIGUORI

Presider: Let us pray that we will receive in full measure the heritage left us by our Father Alphonsus:

Speaker 1: Alphonsus, you struggled to reconcile love of family with the call of the gospel.
All: Bless all families and may their love flow beyond the home to touch the stranger and the alien.

Speaker 2: Alphonsus, you were a lawyer and struggled to makes ideals of justice real in the world.
All: Bless all lawyers and all who work to make the world a place of liberty and justice for all.

Speaker 3: Alphonsus, you were a poet, artist, and musician.
All: May the beauty of this earth widen our hearts to know the God of Loveliness.

Speaker 4: Alphonsus, your whole life was dedicated to preaching the Gospel to the poor.
All: Open our ears to the goodness of Jesus and our mouths to proclaim his mercy.

Speaker 5: Alphonsus, you lived as a brother in community with your Redemptorist confreres.
All: May joy and understanding, forgiveness and peace, reign in our communities and our hearts.

Speaker 6: Alphonsus, all your life you knew the companionship of Mary, the Mother of the Redeemer.
All: May Mary accompany us on our pilgrim way of faith.

The presider invites members of the group to add their own spontaneous petitions to the above.

The Our Father

Presider: United with Saint Alphonsus, we pray as Jesus taught us:

The assembly joins in singing the Our Father.

Closing

Presider: Alphonsus's experience of God caused him to question many things that his church and society took for granted. Alphonsus had the courage to ask: Why can't laypeople grow in intimacy with God through deep prayer? Why is the Church so harsh with human weakness? Why are church workers more concerned about their careers than with the proclamation of the Gospel? Alphonsus knew that a good question is a blessing from God. As a blessing on this feast of our Father Alphonsus, please take a question from the basket and let the life and example of Alphonsus challenge you. While the basket is passed, let us sing the "*Salve Regina*" and recall Alphonsus great love of Mary, the peasant girl of Nazareth, who once questioned and angel of God and Asked, "How can this be?" Let us now sing the "*Salve Regina.*"

All: *The assembly joins in singing the "Salve Regina." The words may be found on page 57.*

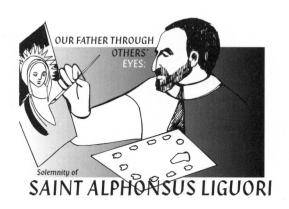

ALPHONSIAN QUESTIONS

These questions are to be copied on another piece of paper so that there are enough copies for each person to take one.

1. Alphonsus had a lifelong focus on a single project—a ceaseless search to bring the good news of God's love to the spiritually abandoned poor. How are we evangelized by the poor in situations of real poverty and misery?

2. Alphonsus's heart was so moved by the poor that he chose to dedicate his energies to change structures of oppression and injustice that maintained poverty. How are we analyzing and actively responding to the global realities and economic and political systems that create and maintain poverty today?

3. Alphonsus cherished his priestly role as reconciler. How are our lives sacraments of reconciliation and songs of God's tender forgiveness?

4. Musician, artist, and poet, Alphonsus believed that the arts could lead people to God. How do we utilize the arts and the artist within each of us to lead others to God?

5. Spiritual director to many through letters and conversations, Alphonsus led countless others to deepened experiences of God's love, often giving the advice, "Empty your heart so that it may be filled with the love of God." How are we called to encourage others to empty their hearts and be filled with God?

LIVING MEMORY OF THE REDEEMER: MARIA CELESTE CROSTAROSA

Environment: A picture of Maria Celeste is surrounded by nine small candles; also part of the display is a basket in which are cards with sayings of Maria Celeste. These quotations are given on page 86.

Opening Song

"Praise, My Soul, the King of Heaven": *Worship #530*
"God Is My Great Desire": *Worship #581*
"Love Divine, All Loves Excelling": *Worship #588*
"Joyful, Joyful, We Adore You": *Gather Comprehensive #528*
"You Are the Voice": *Gather Comprehensive #549*
"Eye Has Not Seen": *Gather Comprehensive #638*

Call to Prayer

Presider: We gather today to celebrate the birthday of our sister, Maria Celeste Crostarosa. Her life's aim was to be a *viva memoria*, a living memory, of the person and mission of Jesus Christ. Like Jesus, she longed for the coming of God's reign above all else. Like Jesus, she knew the pain and the privilege of self-emptying love. Like Jesus, she lives forever in the lives and memories of the Redemptoristines and Redemptorists, laymen and laywomen who are the heirs of her spiritual legacy.

Nine candles, symbolizing the nine virtues that are central to Celeste's spirituality, are arranged in the center of the room. One candle is lit as the section for each virtue is read.

Presider: The spirituality of Maria Celeste revolves around nine virtues, nine energies, through which the Spirit of God grows in us; nine for the nine months of pregnancy— of passage from dark hiddenness in the womb to the light of day. We pray the gospel texts that inspired her; we listen to the words of her Rule, words which she puts on the lips of Jesus.

All: *Virtue 1: Union and Mutual Charity.* "This is my command, that you love one another, as I have loved you. Greater love than this no one has than to lay down one's life for a friend."

Reader 1: Dedicate your body and all your senses for the benefit of your neighbor, your eyes to behold their needs and never to gaze on their defects; your ears to listen to their troubles; your mouth to console them in their afflictions, to defend and to help them.

All: *Virtue 2: Poverty.* "Those who do not renounce everything they have are not worthy to be my disciples."

Reader 2: I was born in a stable; I was an exile in a foreign land. I lived an ordinary life, making my living by labor in Joseph's shop. I went about preaching and I and my disciples were supported on the generosity of others. I lived in the open air, just like a poor beggar. In the end, I died on the wood of the cross with no comfort.

All: *Virtue 3: Purity.* "Blessed are the poor of heart for they shall see God."

Reader 3: Those who are pure of heart shall know God because they gaze fixedly and with loving affection on the Eternal Sun of Justice. They are like eagles who gaze on their goal without ever blinking, so strong is their love.

All: *Virtue 4: Obedience.* "I have come down from heaven not to do my own will but the will of the One who sent me."

Reader 4: As the three divine Persons are one God in the divine unity, so shall you have but one will: the will of Christ, God-made-flesh.

All: *Virtue 5: Humility and Meekness of Heart.* "Learn of me for I am meek and humble of heart."

Reader 5: Humility is first of all living in spirit and in truth.

All: *Virtue 6: Mortification.* "Whoever grasps life will loose it; whoever lets go of life for the sake of the gospel will save it."

Reader 6: Live in my flesh, made holy and mortified for you; live united in my body like branches united to the vine.

All: *Virtue 7: Recollection and Silence.* "I will lead her into the desert and speak to her heart."

Reader 7: The human heart is the throne of God; it is the hidden chest where God places all treasures.

All: *Virtue 8: Prayer.* "You must pray always and never loose heart."

Reader 8: If you wish to imitate me, remember that for me all of life is prayer. Prayer was my continual activity—loving God with the same love with which God loved me.

All: *Virtue 9: Self-Denial and Love of the Cross.* "Whoever wishes to come after me must deny the self, take up the cross and come after me."

Reader 9: O with what love I embraced the cross; I loved it; I desired it; I took pleasure in it—all for your love.

Presider: Celeste wrote that God is our mother and that we are carried and nourished in the womb of God. We now pray in silence to rest and be nourished in the womb of God.

Silent Meditation

The group silently meditates on the nine virtues just described.

Faith-Sharing

The group, at this point, shares impressions of Maria Celeste and her spirituality.

Intercessions

Presider: Celeste wished above all else to be a *viva memoria* of the person and mission of Jesus…

All: May all Christians make the Gospel of Jesus the rule and pattern of their lives.

Presider: Alphonsus was an intimate friend of Celeste and kept all her letters until the end of his life…

All: May we learn to esteem the gift of friendship and to nurture our friendships by gestures of concern and affection.

Presider: Celeste was often visited by Saint Gerard with whom she shared the riches of her spiritual experience…

All: May we be able to strengthen one another by the sharing of our faith.

Presider: When Celeste could not find a suitable priest as spiritual director for her sisters she said to them, "Show the wounds of your spirit to me and together we will find healing…"

All: May the Spirit lead the Church to open itself to the gifts of women as teachers of prayer, as leaders of worship, as ministers of reconciliation.

Presider: Celeste's spirit lives on in our Redemptoristine Sisters. We pray for the community at… (*here the Redemptoristines may be mentioned by name*).

All: May God fill them with many blessings and fullness of peace.

The presider invites members of the assembly to add their own spontaneous petitions to these intercessions.

The Our Father

Presider: We sing together the words our Holy Redeemer gave us.

All: *The assembly sings the Our Father in unison.*

Ritual

Presider: Celeste was the mystic who remembered. As we leave this place of prayer we carry with us some of her words to ponder in our hearts and to enflesh in our lives.

A basket is passed containing papers on which are written a phrase of Maria Celeste. Each person takes one.

Closing Prayer

Presider: Let us conclude our prayer saying together the words of our sister Celeste:

All: This morning You have sounded
the voice of goodness in my soul.
My spirit rejoices in never-ending song.
O Eternal Word, the cause
    of endless eternity!
You are peace, unity, joy, solitude.
O bountiful Joy, who can express the
    fullness of good and contentment
You have given my heart.
O my God, you love Jesus with
    an infinite love
and in you, my Jesus, God loves everyone,
O my bountiful Morning Joy.

MARIA CELESTE CROSTAROSA

LIVING MEMORY OF THE REDEEMER

Here are the words of María Celeste Crostarosa to be recorded on slips of paper and put in a basket.

1. O what an infinite nobility the human soul has! Just thinking about it puts me into an awe-filled silence.

2. Enter into my heart and behold the beauty of the image I have created in my own likeness.

3. When I embrace you in love, I bind you to myself and I also bind you to all other people and them to you.

4. Be a friend of the poor and the humble and never look down on anyone in their littleness for in my kingdom the truly great are those who have loved.

5. You already know, my dear delight, that nothing gives me more pleasure than to heal my wounded members who are poor sinners. Have confidence in me and you can do this very healing with the help of my grace.

6. I love you for what you already are and for what you shall yet become.

7. On the cross a door was cut open for you into my heart so that you may always find entrance there.

8. I want you to possess the joy of my good pleasure in every created thing. My good pleasure will be your bed, your food, our home, your very life, your spirit, your desire, your hope, your security.

9. Do not be afraid. When my spirit rests in the souls of a person it is never silent.

MARIA CELESTE CROSTAROSA

LIVING MEMORY OF THE REDEEMER

THE HOPE OF THE HARVEST IS IN THE SEED: PRAYER FOR THE FEAST OF BLESSED KASPAR STANGASSINGER

Environment: In a central location are positioned the following: a picture of Blessed Kaspar; photographs of formation houses, famous formators in the history of the province or of current formators; photographs or list of names of current students; seeds of mint, parsley, and oregano.

Opening Song

"Faith of Our Fathers": *Worship* #571
"Lord, Whose Love in Humble Service": *Worship* #630
"Now Thank We All Our God": *Gather Comprehensive* #565
"Here I Am Lord": *Gather Comprehensive* #686

Invitation to Prayer

Presider: Our Brother Kaspar delighted in the law of the Lord and found his vocation in teaching it. With him, we praise God and say together:

All: *(Psalm 19)*

The law of the Lord is perfect,
it gives refreshment to the soul.
God's commandments are worthy of trust.
They give wisdom to the simple.
The precepts of the Lord are right,
rejoicing the heart.
The command of the Lord is clear,
giving light to the eye.
The fear of the Lord is pure,
it endures forever.

The statutes are true.
all of them are just;
They are more desirable than gold,
than a hoard of the purest gold.
Sweeter are they than honey,
than honey dripping from the comb.
Let the words of my mouth
and the thoughts of my heart
win favor with you,
Lord, my rock, my redeemer.
Amen.

Readings

Presider: The following readings are from the writings of Blessed Kaspar Stangassinger. Each will be read by a different person in turn with a brief pause between the readings.

Reader 1: Deep is the peace of those who let God enter their hearts.

Reader 2: The saints became holy by doing little things with great love. The littlest things become great when done for God.

Reader 3: The goodness of God is so much greater than we imagine.

Reader 4: Christ will never ask us to die on the cross as he did but he does ask me to love with the same love that led him to die there.

Reader 5: If you speak from your heart, you will draw the hearts of others to you.

Reader 6: For me people are neither Greeks nor Romans; they are Christ.

Faith-Sharing

Presider: *The presider invites members of the group to share a memory of someone who fostered their vocation during their time of discernment or formation and to discuss what quality of this person they would want for themselves.*

Intercessions

Presider: Kaspar dreamed of the missions in Brazil but was sent to teach in the minor seminary. We recall with gratitude all those who postponed their own dreams to serve the needs of the Congregation.

Presider: We remember N. *(here name the novice masters in the history of the province).*
All: May the seeds they planted become a harvest of holiness and zeal.

Presider: We remember N. *(here name teachers and prefects).*
All: May their teaching make us wise.

Presider: We remember N. *(here name brothers who served in our formation houses).*
All: Their lives of hidden devotion nourished and warmed us and gave us a home.

Presider: We remember N. *(here name vocation directors).*
All: May God strengthen their belief in our future.

Presider: We pray for the Redemptorists of the future, whose names we do not know, whose faces we cannot see.
All: May God guide our brothers into whose hands we will entrust our precious Redemptorist heritage.

Ritual

Presider: *The presider invites the members of the assembly to extend their hands in blessing over a tray of herb seeds of parsley, oregano, parsley, and so on. These should later be planted in the community garden or in a window box in the kitchen or refectory.*

The presider then invites the assembly to pray.

> Let us pray in blessing over the new life hidden in these seeds. They will grow into herbs, ordinary plants but useful and strongly flavored. They symbolize ourselves and our future. May those who come after us be, as we have tried to be, ordinary, useful, and strong, green with life.

All extend their hands while the presider prays:

Presider: Blessed are you, God Creator, who has given our Congregation life and growth and abundant fruit.

All: Blessed be God, giver of growth.

Presider: Blessed are you, Jesus Redeemer. By your dying and rising you made even the grave the womb of new life.

All: Blessed be God, giver of growth.

Presider: Blessed are you God the Spirit, wild and free, your energy surges through creation.

All: Blessed be God, giver of growth.

Presider: Let us pray.

All: Holy God, you called Blessed Kaspar, our brother, to follow Jesus the Redeemer as a teacher and friend of youth. By his prayers, keep us faithful to our vocation, hopeful in our future, forever young. Amen.

Closing Antiphon

Presider: Let us now end this prayer service by singing the "*Salve Regina.*" The words to this antiphon may be found on page 57.

PRAYER FOR THE FEAST OF

THE HOPE OF THE HARVEST IS IN THE SEED

BLESSED KASPAR STANGASSINGER

TO LIVE IN THE FREEDOM OF TRUTH: ALFRED PAMPALON

Environment: Prominently displayed in a central spot are the following: a picture of Pampalon; picture of Our Mother of Perpetual Help; flag of Quebéc, a maple leaf or other symbol of Canada; symbols or photographs of various addictions—substance addictions, addiction to consumption, power, control, and so forth.

Opening Song

"There's a Wideness in God's Mercy": *Worship #595*
"We Shall Overcome": *Gather Comprehensive #724*

Call to Prayer

Presider: Alfred Pampalon follows in the tradition of Redemptorist holiness begun on this continent by John Neumann and Francis Seelos and countless other confreres who walked Alphonsus's way of holiness but whose names are forgotten to us. Pampalon, born in 1867 and died in 1896, lived a brief nine years in the Congregation. After a few years of ministry in Belgium and in Canada, Alfred contracted tuberculosis. After terrible sufferings, he died at Sainte Anne de Beaupré on September 30, 1896. His life was unremarkable—a typical Redemptorist life of action and contemplation. The memory of Pampalon was rescued from oblivion by the devotion of the common people. Pilgrims to his tomb in the crypt of Sainte Anne de Beaupré have claimed Pampalon as an intercessor for those struggling with addictions. They see their own struggles with addictions mirrored in his own struggle to suffer the ravages of tuberculosis without painkillers. Anne Wilson Schaef defines an addiction as "anything we feel we have to lie about. If there is something we are not willing to give up in order to make our lives fuller and more healthy, it can probably be classified as an addiction." We pray with our confrere Alfred for the grace to struggle with our own addictions and to live in the freedom of the truth.

Readings and Responses

Reader 1: Jesus said to those who believed in him: "If you obey my teaching, you are really my disciples. You will know the truth and the truth will set you free."

All: The truth will set you free.

Reader 2: Alfred practiced great simplicity of life and wished, as he said, "to be poor out of love for the poor man Jesus." We pray for freedom from an addiction to consumption.

All: The truth will set you free.

Reader 3: Alfred loved the *Magnificat*. He prayed it in the pulpit before every sermon and sang it with his last breath on his deathbed. Mary sings of the God who puts down the mighty from their thrones and raises up the lowly. We pray for freedom from our addiction to power and control.

All: The truth will set you free.

Reader 4: From his days as a student, Alfred was known as "the peacemaker." He wrote, "I will be happy if I live in peace with all my confreres. I will obtain peace if I love them in God whose image they are." We pray for freedom from our addiction to violence.

All: The truth will set you free.

Reader 5: Alfred was a person of a deep interior life. He loved the liturgy and was faithful to many devotions to the Blessed Sacrament, Our Lady, Saint Joseph, Saint Anne, and Saint Alphonsus. We pray for freedom from our addiction to activity that prevents us from cultivating the inner life.

All: The truth will set you free.

Reader 6: On his deathbed, Alfred refused morphine because he did not want to dull his ability to experience all of life. We pray for freedom from our addiction to substances that prevent us from living fully in the truth.

All: The truth will set you free.

Faith-Sharing

Presider: Anne Wilson Schaef gives the following characteristics of addiction and addictive systems: denial; confusion about what is going on; self-centeredness; dishonesty; perfectionism; scarcity model (belief that there is not enough of good things to go around); the illusion of control; frozen feelings; ethical deterioration leading to spiritual bankruptcy. Do we see evidences of these signs of addiction in our community/ Congregation/Church? What can we do to live more fully in the freedom of the truth?

The presider now invites the group to share answers to the preceding questions either with each other or with the group.

Intercessions

Presider: Recognizing our dependence on God's limitless bounty, we make our needs known with confidence.
All: Bountiful God, hear our prayer.

Presider: For God's blessing on the country of Canada and the Province of Saint Anne de Beaupré where Alfred Pampalon walked the way of discipleship, we pray.
All: Bountiful God, hear our prayer.

Presider: For courage and strength for those who struggle in recovery from addictions.
All: Bountiful God, hear our prayer.

Presider: For people in Twelve-Step Programs that through surrender to God and the support of the community they might find the sobriety and serenity for which they long.
All: Bountiful God, hear our prayer.

Presider: For all those who are victims of abuse and violence that they might find healing and support from the community of believers.
All: Bountiful God, hear our prayer.

Presider: That young people will be inspired by the example of Alfred Pampalon to follow Jesus the Redeemer in the family of Saint Alphonsus Liguori.
All: Bountiful God, hear our prayer.

Presider: For the intentions of all those pilgrims who visit the tomb of Alfred Pampalon that they might leave with a deepened sense of God's presence and care.

All: Bountiful God, hear our prayer.

The presider invites members of the assembly to add their own spontaneous petitions.

Closing Prayer

Presider: Let us pray together the Serenity Prayer, the prayer special to all those who struggle to walk in the freedom of the truth:

All: God, grant me the serenity
   to accept the things I cannot change;
   Courage to change the things I can;
   And the wisdom to know the difference.

Closing Canticle

Presider: Alfred Pampalon would keep a small picture of Our Mother of Perpetual Help in the pulpit whenever he would preach and would silently pray the *Magnificat* before every sermon. We conclude our prayer by singing Mary's song of praise. We pray that her vision of a world where the humble are raised up and the empty filled will direct our energies and our actions.

The prayer concludes with the assembly singing any version of the Magnificat, *the traditional Gregorian chant or the version in* Gather Comprehensive #14 *or* #788.

18

SERVE THE LORD WITH JOY: BLESSED FRANCIS X. SEELOS

Environment: Picture of Francis Seelos and a mirror surrounded by candles/flowers displayed in a central spot.

Opening Song

"Sing to the Lord a Joyful Song": *Worship #532*

Call to Prayer

Presider: We see in the life of Francis Seelos a mirror of our own Redemptorist life. Like us he experienced a number of transfers from one community to another: Pittsburgh, Baltimore, Cumberland, Annapolis, New Orleans. He was called to change ministries several times—formator, missionary, parish priest. He lived with saints like John Neumann; he lived with confreres like Gabriel Rumpler who suffered from mental illness. In the midst of it all, he struggled to live a life of holiness, serenity, and joy. We pray that we who share his life will know his contentment in following the Most Holy Redeemer. He was called by Father Ruland, "a Redemptorist in body and soul." As we listen to his words, we pray to be the same.

Readings

Reader 1: It is not your justice but God's mercy which is the motive of your trust. He is the God of all consolations and the Father of mercies. He does not wish the death of sinners, but that they be converted and live. He came to heal the sick and to seek those who were lost. He spared the woman taken in adultery. He showed mercy to the thief crucified with him. He took upon himself our punishment. He prayed for his murderers. He now intercedes for us at the right hand of God. None of the damned was ever lost because his sin was too great, but because his trust was too small!

Pause for Silent Meditation

Reader 2: Want of urbanity effects no good and affability does no evil. The priest who is rough with people does injury to himself and to others; he sins, at least in ignorance, against charity, patience, poverty, humility, and self-denial. He scandalizes all who see him and hear him. Hundreds of souls turn away him, from God and from religion. Thousands reject the Church and the sacraments and perish in eternity solely because they have been badly treated by a priest.

Pause for Silent Meditation

Reader 3: A long experience has taught me the great lesson that God leads men in a human manner by other men whom he appointed to be in his place and who should be of the same kindness as he himself was while on earth. Many a soul might be gained for the true faith and eternal life if sometimes a little more charity, a little more self-denial, would be evident, and if persons would be treated as their personal dispositions and human nature would require. It is true that it requires great virtue and experience to find always the right measure in these things, but we cannot fail much if our intention remains pure.

Pause for Silent Meditation

Psalm Response

Presider: Let us now pray the following psalm together.

All: Praise the Lord, my soul;
    I will praise the Lord all my days;
    I will praise my God as long as I live.
    Happy are those whose help is the God of Jacob,
    whose hope is in the Lord their God.
    God is maker of heaven and earth,
    the seas and all that is in them.
    God keeps faith forever,
    secures justice for the oppressed,
    gives food to the hungry.
    God sets the captives free,
    God gives sight to the blind.
    God raises up those who are bowed low;
    the Lord loves the righteous.
    God protects the stranger,
    sustains the orphan and the widow

but thwarts the plans of the wicked.
God will reign forever,
your God, Zion, through all generations.
Alleluia!

Faith-Sharing

Presider: Let us now share with each other or with the group as a whole an experience in each of your lives when anger was overcome by gentleness, anger diffused by humor, or violence calmed by peace.

Ritual

Presider: As I pass the mirror around the room, I invite you each to take the mirror and to look for a few moments at your reflection and pray silently that the virtues of Father Seelos will be yours: patience, kindness, and joy in God's service.

The mirror is passed through the assembly. Soft instrumental music may be played during this ritual.

Intercessions

Presider: In one of his conferences, Father Seelos quotes Saint John Chrysostom who says, "Even if you do not bend the knee, nor strike your breast nor elevate your hands toward heaven, if only you bring to God an inflamed heart, nothing is wanting in your prayer." Let us bring our inflamed hearts to God in prayer for our own needs and those of the whole world. Our response to each of the following intercessions is "Inflame our hearts with your love!"

Presider: For confessors and pastoral counselors, for reconcilers and peacemakers, for those who, like Father Seelos, work to bring rest to troubled minds and peace to a broken world, we pray…
All: Inflame our hearts with your love.

Presider: For doctors and nurses, for medical researchers and scientists, for those who, like Father Seelos, try to relieve the victims of disease and bring them healing and wholeness, we pray…
All: Inflame our hearts with your love.

Presider: For comedians and clowns, writers and artists, who, like Father Seelos, try to relieve the sadness of life by humor and good cheer, we pray…

All: Inflame our hearts with your love.

Presider: For teachers and youth ministers, who, like Father Seelos, try to accompany young people with patience and care, we pray…
All: Inflame our hearts with your love.

Presider: For growth in kindness and courtesy, for the everyday virtues for which Father Seelos was famous, we pray…
All: Inflame our hearts with your love.

Presider: For peace among nations and within our borders, for a healing of the divisions in our society which Father Seelos witnessed during the Civil War, we pray…
All: Inflame our hearts with your love.

Presider: For those who are alienated from God or the Church because of the unkindness of believers, we pray…
All: Inflame our hearts with your love.

Presider: Let us now add spontaneous petitions of our own to these intercessions.

The Hail Mary

Presider: Father Seelos wrote, "O Mary, Mother of Mercy! You understood the Mercy of God when you cried out in the *Magnificat*: 'His Mercy is from generation to generation.' Obtain for all sinners a childlike confidence in the Mercy of God!" And so we pray:
All: *The assembly prays the Hail Mary in unison.*

Blessing

Presider: Let us extend our hands in blessing toward the world and be mindful of all those who feel separated from God and alienated from the Church as we listen to the words of Father Seelos: "Oh, if only all the sinners of the whole wide world were present here! Yes, even the greatest, the most hardened, even those close to despair, I would call out to them:
All: "The Lord is kind and merciful, patient and full of love."

FRANCIS XAVIER SEELOS

SERVE THE LORD WITH JOY

SAINT TERESA OF ÁVILA: ALL ON FIRE

Environment: A display including an image or picture of Teresa, copies of some of her writings, a tambourine or castanets (instruments she loved to play), map of Spain, one large candle and enough smaller vigil lights for each participant. These can be placed on a piece of orange cloth—Teresa's favorite color.

Opening Song

"As a Fire Is Meant for Burning": *Gather Comprehensive #663*

Call to Prayer

Presider: We rejoice to celebrate the memory of our mother Saint Teresa of Ávila. A patron of our Congregation from the beginning, she was dearly loved by Saint Alphonsus and one of his earliest works was about her spirituality. He called her his second mother and his greatest teacher of prayer. Her name appeared with that of Jesus, Mary, and Joseph at the top of every paper to which he set his pen. Alphonsus called her, "a woman all on fire with God's love." Let us draw near to her in prayer to be warmed by her spirit.

Pause for Silent Prayer

Presider: We pray together to Teresa in the words of Saint Alphonsus:
All: O woman aflame like a seraph, Teresa,
  beloved spouse of Jesus Crucified,
  you burned with such great love of God while on earth;
  you burn now with an even brighter flame in heaven.
  You wished for nothing more than that all people would love God.
  By your prayer obtain for me too a spark of that holy fire.
  May all my thoughts, desires, and affections be devoted to seeking
  the will of our Good God who so deserves my unbounded love.

Keep me faithful in the midst of joys and sorrows.

Obtain for me this grace, Teresa,

you who are so close to God,

to be all on fire, as were you, with God's own love. Amen.

Readings

Presider: Let us listen, as Alphonsus did, to the words of Teresa, the great teacher of prayer:

Each of the following quotes from the works of Teresa are read by a different person in turn. There should be a pause between each quote.

Reader 1: God doesn't force our will. God takes whatever we give but God doesn't give himself completely until we give ourselves completely.

Reader 2: I tried as hard as I could to keep Jesus Christ, our God and Lord, present within me. That was my way of prayer.

Reader 3: We shouldn't build castles in the air. God doesn't look so much at the greatness of our works as at the love with which they are done.

Reader 4: If contemplating, taking care of the sick, helping with the household chores, are all ways of serving the Guest who comes to be with us as we eat and recreate, what difference does it make whether we serve in the one way or the other?

Reader 5: Some will tell you that speaking with a friend is unnecessary, that it is enough to have God. But I think that a good means to having God is to speak with his friends.

Reader 6: Many remain at the foot of the mount who could ascend to the top. I repeat and ask that you always have courageous thoughts. As a result of them the Lord will give you grace for courageous deeds.

Reader 7: I do not understand the fears of those who are afraid to begin mental prayer. I do not know what they are afraid of. Prayer is nothing but a friendly conversation with the God who we know loves us.

Presider: It is easy to see how the spirit of Teresa resonated deeply with that of Alphonsus. Let us now spend some time in silence, in friendly conversation with the God who loves us.

The assembly pauses for an extended period of silent prayer.

Faith-Sharing

Presider: Let each member of the assembly share with a neighbor or with the group as a whole a response to these questions: Why do you think the figure of Teresa of Ávila was so attractive to Saint Alphonsus? What quality of Teresa is it important for Redemptorists today to recapture?

Ritual

The presider lights his vigil light with the flame of the large candle. The flame passes through the room, each lighting his neighbor's candle and saying as he does so the words of Alphonsus's prayer to Teresa: "Be all on fire with God's love."

Intercessions

Presider: Teresa tells us that, as God never tires of giving, we ought never to tire of receiving. Let these flames which we hold be symbols of our desire to see God known and loved by all. Let us make our needs known to God and respond to the petitions in the words of Teresa: "Nothing is lacking to the one who has God; God alone suffices."

Presider: That all Redemptorists will share the love of Alphonsus for Teresa of Ávila and will grow in her spirit of prayer and her passion for the reign of God, we pray…
All: Nothing is lacking to the one who has God; God alone suffices.

Presider: For all teachers of prayer and spiritual directors that they will be inspired by the example and writings of Teresa, we pray…
All: Nothing is lacking to the one who has God; God alone suffices.

Presider: For all who love beauty as Teresa did and celebrate the goodness of life through art, music, and dance, we pray…
All: Nothing is lacking to the one who has God; God alone suffices.

Presider: For all those who feel themselves far from God, that they will discover God's hidden presence in their darkness, we pray…

All: Nothing is lacking to the one who has God; God alone suffices.

Presider: I invite those of you who wish to add spontaneous petitions of your own to these intercessions.

At the conclusion of the petitions the presider invites all to place their candles around the picture of Teresa.

The Our Father

Presider: Teresa advised those who had difficulties in prayer simply to repeat the Our Father as slowly as possible and to try to enter into the spirit of the words. Let us end our prayer in that way, silently praying the words that Jesus gave us.

The assembly recites the Our Father in unison.

ALL ON FIRE:
Saint Teresa of Ávila

FOOL FOR LOVE:
SAINT GERARD MAJELLA

Environment: In a central place, set up a display that includes a picture or statue of Saint Gerard with flowers and candles; needle, thread and cloth (symbols of Gerard as tailor); and a picture of a pregnant woman or a baby symbolizing Gerard as patron of expectant mothers.

Invitation to Prayer

Presider: May the God whom Gerard Majella called the "thief of hearts" be with you.
All: May God's love possess our hearts forever.

Opening Song

Presider: When Gerard was porter in Caposele an extraordinary incident took place. Among the poor who crowded for alms at the monastery door was a blind man, Philip di Falcone, who played the flute well and sang excellently. Philip and his dog were well known to Gerard and were always sure of getting a welcome and a bite to eat from him. One day Gerard saw Philip in the crowd at the monastery door and asked him to play something. "What do you wish me to play?" asked the blind man. Gerard asked him to play an Italian air set to the words of a hymn written by Saint Alphonsus. On hearing the first words of the hymn, Gerard clapped his hands and danced with joy:

All listen to the hymn "Il mio gusto"; a translation appears below:

Your good pleasure, not my own.
In you, my God, I love alone;
And nothing I desire of you
But what your goodness wills for me.
O will of God! O will divine!
All, all our love be ever yours.

In love no rival can you bear,
But you are full of tenderest care;
And fire and sweetness all divine
To hearts which are wholly yours.
O will of God! O will divine!
All, all our love be ever yours.

You make crosses soft and light
And death itself seems sweet and bright.
No cross nor fear that soul dismays
Whose will to you united stays.
O will of God! O will divine!
All, all our love be ever yours.

Scripture Reading

Reader 1: This is a reading from the Letter to the Romans: 8:31–39.

All: *The assembly responds with the following refrain from* Gather Comprehensive #593:
We remember how you loved us to your death,
and still we celebrate for you are with us here;
And we believe that we will see you when you come, in your glory, Lord.
We remember, we celebrate, we believe.

Readings From Saint Gerard

Presider: One of Gerard's contemporaries said of him, "Every word of his was an arrow that went straight to the heart." Let us listen to the words of our Brother Gerard and let his words touch our hearts. Each line will be read by a different person in turn.

Speaker 1: "Life for me is faith. All we do for God is a prayer."

Speaker 2: "The sick and the poor are Jesus Christ visible. The Blessed Sacrament is Jesus Christ invisible."

Speaker 3: "The poor are living images of Jesus Christ. It is we who have sinned and it is the innocent poor who suffer for it."

Speaker 4: "I recreate myself in the immensity of God."

Speaker 5: "Mary, I wish to love you as much as Jesus Christ loves you."

Speaker 6: "I will never accuse anyone or speak of the faults of anyone, even in jest. I will always excuse my neighbor, seeing in him the person of Jesus unjustly accused. Should anyone speak ill of another, I will warn him of his fault, even though he is our Rector Major himself."

Speaker 7: "When I know or hear of anyone who is being greatly tried by the Divine Will and has no longer the courage to suffer and ask for divine help, I will pray to God for him for three whole days at least and offer up all I do in order to obtain for him holy conformity with God's will."

Response

All: O my God, I wish to convert as many sinners
    as there are grains of sand in the sea and on the land,
    as there are leaves on the trees,
    blades of grass in the fields,
    atoms in the air,
    stars in the sky,
    rays in the sun and moon,
    creatures on the whole earth.

Faith-Sharing

Presider: Let each one of us now share an impression of Saint Gerard or a quality of his one would want for oneself.

Intercessions

Presider: Gerard loved to call himself a fool for love.
All: May we be willing to risk everything for the sake of the Gospel of Jesus Christ.

Presider: Gerard was a woodcarver who released images of the Crucified Redeemer hidden in pieces of wood.
All: May we grow in faith that the power of the dying and rising of Jesus moves hidden in the history of our world.

Presider: Gerard loved the feast of Pentecost above all others; the day of Wind and Flame.
All: May the wind of the Spirit give us new energy; the flame of the Spirit renewed enthusiasm.

Presider: Gerard cupped the hands of a peasant girl in his to form a chalice of warmth.
All: May our communities and ministries be places of welcome and hospitality.

Presider: Gerard was a tailor who stitched fabrics together to make useful garments.
All: May we repair the torn fabric of the frayed edges of our world and make the earth whole again.

Presider: Gerard was a skilled spiritual director and a preacher of conversion.
All: May we always approach the conscience of another with delicacy and reverence.

Presider: I now invite anyone who wishes to add his or her own spontaneous petitions to the intercessions above.

The Our Father

Presider: We now pray together as Jesus taught us:
All: *The assembly prays the Our Father in unison.*

Closing Prayer

Presider: Let us pray. Wonder-working God, you placed treasure in earthen vessels and have impressed your image in the fragile clay of the children of the earth. You raised up Gerard Majella as a healer, a friend of the sinner and the poor, as a fool for love. By his prayers, may we, his brothers, become more faithful disciples of Jesus who came not to be served but to serve. We make this prayer in his name, Jesus the Most Holy Redeemer.
All: Amen.

Blessing

Presider: Gerard was once released from a great trial of desolation when Dominic Blassuci made the sign of the cross over his heart. As a final blessing, I invite you to trace the sign of the Redeemer over one another's hearts.

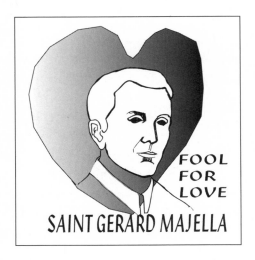

FOOL FOR LOVE

SAINT GERARD MAJELLA

DOES NOT YOUR HEART SPEAK? PRAYER SERVICE FOR THE FOUNDATION OF THE CONGREGATION

November 9

Environment: The prayer service takes place in a church or chapel. The altar is the central symbol of the prayer and may be suitably decorated.

Opening Song

"Come, Holy Ghost": *Worship #482*
"Veni Creator Spiritus": *Worship #479*

Invitation to Prayer

Presider: Praised be the God and Father of Our Lord Jesus Christ, who has chosen us in Christ, before the world began…

All: To be holy and blameless in his sight, to be full of love.

Reading

Reader: Alphonsus spent nearly two years in discernment between his first encounter with the abandoned poor of Scala and the founding of the Congregation on November 9, 1732. During this time, Falcoia wrote to him, recalling his experience with the abandoned poor and urging him to act: "The Lord wants you, in fact he has chosen you as one of the foundation stones of this edifice. I cannot understand your reasons for doubting this. Does not your heart speak to you? Does not a situation which requires you to embrace what is most deeply felt within you and to follow the great master who leads you, reassure you?"

Alphonsus listened to the voice of his heart and embraced what was deepest within him. On November 9, 1732, the Congregation was born. The inaugural ceremony was simple: the invocation of the Holy Spirit, asking for God's gifts; the singing of the "*Te Deum*" giving praise and thanks for God's favors; the celebration of the Eucharist, rooting the Congregation in the dying and rising of the Redeemer. Of the six men present that day, only Alphonsus would persevere. They had no financial resources and lived in a rented house. They did not have approval from either the Church or state. They did not even have a name yet, let alone a Rule. All they had was a man who listened to the voice of his heart and embraced what was deepest within him. It was enough.

Intercessions

Presider: Like our first confreres, let us pray for the outpouring of the gifts of the Holy Spirit on our Congregation. May the Spirit enable us to listen to the voice of our hearts and to embrace what is deepest within us. To each of the following petitions, please respond "Come, Holy Spirit."

Presider: With the fire of your love…
All: Come, Holy Spirit.
Presider: With the boldness of your speech…
All: Come, Holy Spirit.
Presider: With the power of your Word…
All: Come, Holy Spirit.
Presider: With the gentleness of your Breath…
All: Come, Holy Spirit.
Presider: With the light of your Truth…
All: Come, Holy Spirit.
Presider: With the transforming power of your wind…
All: Come, Holy Spirit.
Presider: With the shining splendor of your Wisdom…
All: Come, Holy Spirit.
Presider: With your creative energy…
All: Come, Holy Spirit.
Presider: With your ever-present care…
All: Come, Holy Spirit.
Presider: With your gift of prayer…
All: Come, Holy Spirit.
Presider: With your tender mercy…

All: Come, Holy Spirit.

Presider: With your strong consolation…

All: Come, Holy Spirit.

Presider: Let all who wish add additional spontaneous petitions to these intercessions.

Thanksgiving

Presider: Like our first confreres let us praise God's graciousness to our Congregation in the words of the ancient Christian hymn, the *"Te Deum."*

All: *The assembly sings "Holy God, We Praise Thy Name"* (Worship #524).

Presider: Let us give praise and thanks to God who has used us, despite our weaknesses and failures, as instruments to proclaim the good news of plentiful redemption…

All: We praise you. We give you thanks.

Presider: For making us sharers in the ministry of redemption…

All: We praise you. We give you thanks.

Presider: For using us as instruments of peace and reconciliation…

All: We praise you. We give you thanks.

Presider: For the gifts of speech and music, art and craft, organization and leadership among us…

All: We praise you. We give you thanks.

Presider: For the dreams and enthusiasm of our youth…

All: We praise you. We give you thanks.

Presider: For the wisdom and strength of our elders…

All: We praise you. We give you thanks.

Presider: For extending our Congregation to the corners of the earth, enriching us with the gifts of many peoples and nations…

All: We praise you. We give you thanks.

Presider: For the ever-present intercession of Our Mother of Perpetual Help…

All: We praise you. We give you thanks.

Presider: Any member of the group now is welcome to add spontaneous expressions of thanksgiving for God's gifts.

Faith-Sharing

Presider: I now invite members of the assembly to share with their neighbors or with the entire group their responses to these questions:

We are called to refound the Congregation in each generation. Alphonsus was moved by the abandonment of the shepherds of Scala. What situation today calls for the response of our Congregation? What do we hear when we listen to the voice of our hearts? What is deepest within us that we are called to embrace—what elements of our charism do we need to revive in order to do that?

Renewal of Vows

Presider: Before the foundation of the Congregation, the first confreres, together with Father Falcoia and the nuns of Scala, spent three days of prayer before the Blessed Sacrament. The Eucharist is the source from which our Congregation receives its strength. Eucharistic community is the end toward which all our ministries are directed. I invite you to come forward now, to encircle the table of the Lord, and, placing your hands on it, to renew your commitment to follow Jesus the Redeemer in the way of Alphonsus.

The confreres encircle the altar of the church or chapel and place their hands on it.

Presider: Let us pray now in silence and renew our profession in our own words. Does your heart not speak to you and call you to embrace what is deepest within you?

The entire assembly prays silently together.

Presider: In his old age, Alphonsus recalled the grotto of Scala and the beautiful things Our Lady told him about the future of the Congregation. He was sustained all his life by that experience. We are the future which Mary described to Alphonsus. Let us celebrate her presence in our history. Let us sing together the *"Salve Regina."* The words to this antiphon may be found on page 57.

Sign of Peace

Presider: Let us recommit ourselves to one another by offering a sign of peace.

FOUNDATION OF THE CONGREGATION

FIRE CARRYING FIRE: PRAYER FOR THE SOLEMNITY OF THE IMMACULATE CONCEPTION
Patronal Feast of the Congregation

Environment: A display containing the following is set up: an image of the Immaculate Conception or Our Lady of Perpetual Help or any other suitable image of Mary; the paschal candle; one large candle and enough small votive candles for each person in the group.

Opening Song

"Immaculate Mary": *Worship #708*

While the opening song is sung, the large candle is lighted from the paschal candle and placed in front of the image of Mary.

Call to Prayer

Presider: Today, the solemnity of the Immaculate Conception, is the day given by Saint Alphonsus to the Redemptorist Congregation as our patronal feast. Called to proclaim God's plentiful redemption to the poor, we celebrate Mary, the poor woman of Nazareth, in whom the mission of Redemption is realized most fully.

All: Praised be the God and Father
of our Lord Jesus Christ,
who has bestowed on us in Christ
every spiritual blessing in the heavens.
God chose us in Christ,
before the world began,
to be holy and blameless in his sight,
to be full of love.

Presider: Called to the ministry of reconciliation, we celebrate Mary who never lost God's friendship and who works in the Church as a reconciler and peacemaker.

All: May Christ dwell in our hearts through faith
so that, rooted and grounded in love,
we may have the strength to understand with all the holy ones
what is the breadth and length and height and depth
of the love of Christ.

Presider: Called to build up the community of the Church, we celebrate Mary who prays in the midst of the disciples for the full outpouring of the Holy Spirit.

All: When the fullness of time had come,
God sent his Son, born of a woman, born under the law,
to redeem those under the law,
that we might receive adoption.
As proof that we are God's children,
God sent the Spirit into our hearts, crying out
"Abba, Father!"

Reading

Reader: This reading is from *The Glories of Mary* by Saint Alphonsus: "God, who is love, came on earth to enkindle in the hearts of all the flame of divine love. In no heart did he enkindle so much as in that of Mary. Her heart was entirely pure from all earthly affections and fully prepared to burn with this blessed flame. The heart of Mary became all fire and flames as we read of her in the Song of Songs, 'The flames of love are a blazing fire'—fire burning within through love and flames shining outside through the example she gave to all in the practice of virtue. When Mary, then, was in this world, and bore Jesus in her arms, she could well be called 'fire carrying fire.'"

Silent Prayer and Reflection

Presider: The history of our Congregation and the lives of each one of us has been marked by the maternal intercession of the Immaculate Virgin Mary. Let us pray now in silent thanksgiving to God for the ways in which God's love has been shown to us through Mary.

The assembly observes a period of silent reflection.

Consecration to Mary

Each confrere is given a lighted candle to hold during the prayer of consecration. At the end of the prayer each confrere comes forward and places his candle before the image of Mary.

Presider: Let us together consecrate ourselves, our Congregation and its ministries, to the Immaculate Virgin Mary, our Mother of Perpetual Help. Mary, woman of Nazareth, we know and love you under a thousand names:

All: Guadalupe, Aparecida, Fátima and Lourdes, Carmel and Good Counsel, Częstochowa and Knock.

Presider: Especially for us you are Our Mother of Perpetual Help.

All: Your gaze of compassion has accompanied us through life.

Presider: From the walls of our family homes, in houses of formation, on missions, in rectory parlors and from common-room walls.

All: You have been our companion on the pilgrim way of faith.

Presider: Immaculate Mary, Mother of Perpetual Help, obtain for us your faith that the Most High who has done great things in you can work marvels in and through us as well.

Intercessions

All: Immaculate Mary, we consecrate ourselves to you and we entrust to your perpetual help our Congregation, its communities and ministries. As your presence has marked our past, we are full of faith that your intercession guides our future.

Presider: For our missionaries…
All: Be a perpetual help.
Presider: For our formators…
All: Be a perpetual help.
Presider: For our parish ministers…
All: Be a perpetual help.
Presider: For preachers and retreat masters…
All: Be a perpetual help.
Presider: For our provincial government…
All: Be a perpetual help.
Presider: For spiritual directors and confessors…
All: Be a perpetual help.
Presider: For our sick and aging confreres…
All: Be a perpetual help.

Presider: For our novices and students…
All: Be a perpetual help.
Presider: For our families and friends…
All: Be a perpetual help.
Presider: For our benefactors…
All: Be a perpetual help.
Presider: For all God's holy people…
All: Be a perpetual help.

The confreres now place their candles around the image of Mary.

Closing Prayer and Antiphon

Presider: With confidence that God who began this good work in us will bring it to completion, we make Mary's hymn of praise our own.
All: Our souls proclaim the Holy One who dwells within us.
Our spirits rejoice in the presence of God among us.
Because we as Redemptorists have been touched and called.
Generations of believers have known God's blessing through us.
Great things have been done through us and our brothers before us.
"Of the Most Holy Redeemer" is our name.
God has shown mercy through us, from age to age.
We have joined with one another to proclaim good news to the poor,
to bring healing to the brokenhearted with tenderness and care.
We, too, have been hungry and have filled one another with good things.
We have known God's faithfulness and God's promise of redemption.
A promise God made to Alphonsus, Clement, Gerard, John
and to their brothers forever.
Glory be to the God of Loveliness, to the Redeemer Most Holy,
to the Life-Giving Spirit.
As it was in the beginning, is now, and will be forever. Amen.
So we hope; so may it be.
Presider: We now join in singing the "*Salve Regina.*" The words may be found on page 57.

PART THREE

PRAYER ON
REDEMPTORIST
THEMES

WE REMEMBER: A PRAYER SERVICE CELEBRATING ALPHONSIAN SPIRITUALITY

Environment: In a central place in the room can be arranged traditional and/or contemporary symbols of the key themes in the spirituality of Saint Alphonsus: for example, an emblem of the incarnation—an image of the Infant Jesus from a Nativity scene or a photograph of a poor child today; an emblem of the Passion—a crucifix or a photograph of a person or people who are suffering Christ's passion today; an emblem of the Eucharist—a piece of bread and glass of wine, a monstrance, sheaves of wheat and grapes, a photograph of people who are themselves Eucharist for another; an emblem of Mary—a picture of Our Lady of Perpetual Help, one of the Madonnas of Saint Alphonsus, or other traditional image of Mary, a photograph or contemporary image of Mary.

Invitation to Prayer

Presider: May the God who took human flesh in the womb of the Virgin Mary;
   May the God who accompanied us through death to new life;
   May the God who is present among us when we break the bread;
   May the God of Alphonsus Liguori be with you.

All: May the God of Alphonsus live in our hearts forever!

Readings and Responses

Reader 1: This reading is from the Final Document of the Twenty-First General Chapter: "The center of Redemptorist spirituality is Christ the Redeemer, as he reveals himself above all in the mysteries of the Incarnation, Passion and Resurrection which we celebrate in the Eucharist. These lead the Redemptorist to be his living memorial and to continue his mission in the world. This profoundly Christocentric spirituality impels us to recover the heritage of Saint Alphonsus in his "exodus" towards the poor. The Redemptorist follows Christ the Redeemer and pursues his liberating action. Mary is the first disciple of the Redeemer, whom she accepted as the Word of God; she guided us on our journey of identification with him. In her is found the most perfect image of liberation and of liberating activity.

All: *The assembly responds by singing the following refrain from the hymn "We Remember"* (Gather Comprehensive #593) *in unison:*

We remember how you loved us to your death,
and still we celebrate, for you are with us here.
We believe that we will see you when you come in your glory, Lord.
We remember, we celebrate, we believe.

Crib

Reader 2: This reading is from the works of Saint Alphonsus: "O Word made flesh, you are at a loss to know what more you can do to make yourself loved by us. You first appeared among us as a poor child. Even from your birth you lost no time in drawing our hearts to yourself. Make us fall in love with your goodness."

Presider: In the Incarnation, Saint Alphonsus saw a God who shared our life completely.

All: May the example of the Word made flesh inspire us to open ourselves to one another and to make all the struggles of the human family our own.

All: *The assembly responds by singing the following refrain from the hymn "We Remember"* (Gather Comprehensive #593) *in unison:*

We remember how you loved us to your death,
and still we celebrate, for you are with us here.
We believe that we will see you when you come in your glory, Lord.
We remember, we celebrate, we believe.

Cross

Reader 2: This reading is from a letter of Saint Alphonsus dated November 1751: "My brothers, by the grace of God we perform wonders wherever we go on mission. People say they have never before experienced a mission like ours. Why? Because we go by obedience, we go in poverty, and we preach Christ crucified."

Presider: In the paschal mystery, Saint Alphonsus saw Jesus in total commitment to the mission of healing, liberating, and redeeming God's people.

All: May the power of the cross which we preach, renew in each of us our desire to give ourselves without compromise to the mission of the Congregation.

All: *The assembly responds by singing the following refrain from the hymn "We Remember" (Gather Comprehensive #593) in unison:*

We remember how you loved us to your death,
and still we celebrate, for you are with us here.
We believe that we will see you when you come in your glory, Lord.
We remember, we celebrate, we believe.

Eucharist

Reader 3: This is a reading from the works of Saint Alphonsus: "My God, my true and only love. What more could you have done to be loved by us? To die was not enough for you, my Lord. You instituted the Eucharist to give yourself totally to us and to bind yourself, heart to heart, with us. My God, I love you above all things. I wish to see you loved as you deserve."

Presider: Saint Alphonsus devoted his life to building up communities centered around the Eucharist.

All: May our devotion to the Sacrament of Unity empower us to lives of sharing of faith and service with one another and among the people of God.

All: *The assembly responds by singing the following refrain from the hymn "We Remember" (Gather Comprehensive #593) in unison:*

We remember how you loved us to your death,
and still we celebrate, for you are with us here.
We believe that we will see you when you come in your glory, Lord.
We remember, we celebrate, we believe.

Mary

Reader 4: This reading is from the works of Saint Alphonsus: "Mary co-operated by love in the spiritual birth of all the members of the Church. It was on Mount Calvary that Jesus formed the Church and the Virgin Mary co-operated in a special manner in the accomplishment of this work. It was on Calvary that Mary began, in a special way, to be Mother of the whole Church."

Presider: Saint Alphonsus saw Mary as the midwife in the spiritual birth of the Church from the wounded side of the Redeemer.

All: May the prayers of Mary accompany us as we preach the Gospel anew and build the Church of the future.

All: *The assembly responds by singing the following refrain from the hymn "We Remember" (Gather Comprehensive #593) in unison:*

We remember how you loved us to your death,
and still we celebrate, for you are with us here.
We believe that we will see you when you come in your glory, Lord.
We remember, we celebrate, we believe.

Faith-Sharing

Presider: After a few moments of silent reflection, please share with some of the people around you your answer to the following question: Which element of the Redemptorist spiritual tradition is particularly nourishing to you?

Closing Prayer

All: Loving God, we gather today to celebrate the call of Alphonsus Liguori whose faith inspires us in our own commitment to the redeeming mission of Jesus. United in a common heritage, we look to your Spirit, alive in every age, to renew in us the unbounded love of Jesus our Redeemer. May the Spirit draw us more closely to one another, so that the future we build will have no other foundation than Jesus the Redeemer, who is Lord forever and ever. Amen.

FINDING GOD IN THE MAILBOX: REDEMPTORISTS AS SPIRITUAL DIRECTORS

Environment: Each of the readings to be used in this service are placed in a separate envelope and arranged around a candle. At the time for the readings, each reader takes one of the "letters," opens the envelope and reads aloud. There should also be a note card and envelope to give to each of the participants at the conclusion of the service.

Opening Hymn

"Eye Has Not Seen": *Gather Comprehensive #638*
Verses 1 and 2 are sung as the opening hymn; the refrain is sung again between each reading; Verse 3 is sung at the conclusion of the prayer service.

Call to Prayer

Presider: From the beginning of the Christian community the members of the Church used letters to support one another and to guide one another in the ways of the Spirit. From the beginning of our Congregation, Redemptorists have been sought out as guides to life in the Spirit. Often they gave that guidance by letter, in odd moments taken out of a busy missionary life. These letters form a precious heritage of the Redemptorist experience of the workings of God in the human heart. As Benedictine author Macrina Wiederkehr reflects, "Letters are the stories of our souls. Unlike a phone call, a letter can be picked up again and again. It can be deeply pondered. It can be eaten. Always serve letters with a cup of tea and a footstool. Celebrate the reading slowly. It is irreverent to read a letter fast." *A Tree Full of Angels*, San Francisco:HarperSF, 1988). Let us listen reverently first to the word of God in Scripture than to God's workings in our confreres.

Readings and Responses

Reader 1: A reading from the Second Letter of Paul to the Corinthians: "We are not like so many others, who handle God's message as it were cheap merchandise; but because God sent us, we speak with sincerity in his presence as servants of Christ. Does this sound as if we were boasting about ourselves? Could it be that, like some other people, we need letters of recommendation to you or from you? You yourselves are the letter we have, written on our hearts for everyone to know and read. It is clear that Christ himself wrote this letter and sent it by us. It is written, not with ink but with the Spirit of the living God, and not on stone tablets but on human hearts."

All: *The assembly sings the refrain of "Eye Has Not Seen" as a response.*

Reader 2: This letter was written by Alphonsus Liguori to Mother Angiola del Cielo and the nuns of Scala on October 29, 1730: "May Jesus and Mary always possess our hearts! I received your first letters on the feast of my patroness Saint Teresa; it was a consolation for me just to see the envelope, for then I realized who had written those letters. Now that I am writing I want to tell you that even though it has been some time since my visit to Scala, the memory of you is as vivid as if I had only left yesterday. If this seems like I am exaggerating, ask our Lord to help me forget you; because as far as I am concerned, I hope that memory will always be with me; since it draws me closer to God. I want to tell you that the words of your letters help to inflame me with the love of God....I am your most devoted and humble servant, Alfonso de Liguori, a wretched sinner."

All: *The assembly sings the refrain of "Eye Has Not Seen" as a response.*

Reader 3: This is part of a letter from Blessed Gennaro Sarnelli to Mother Maria Angiola del Cielo: "When you are alone in your cells or when you go out on the porch, look at the mountain ranges of Cilento and even farther beyond. Imagine the hundreds and hundreds of mountains that form a chain and imagine the immense population of men and women who live in them, old and young, all abandoned like sheep without a shepherd, who cry out looking for mercy and help....As you look raise your eyes to heaven and address yourself to God and say, "Lord, have mercy on these souls. Stretch out your hands to them and in spirit wrap them in the immense womb of God's goodness."

All: *The assembly sings the refrain of "Eye Has Not Seen" as a response.*

Reader 4: This is from a letter of Cesare Sportelli to Barbara Buonincontro dated October 25, 1745: "In prayer when the soul feels itself drawn to a certain loving quiet in the Lord there present, then rest in your God for as long as it pleases him. When it please God that you meditate or make affections, always be careful not to force yourself but be always peaceful in your prayers for the throne of God is peace."

All: *The assembly sings the refrain of "Eye Has Not Seen" as a response.*

Reader 5: This is from a letter of Father Carmine Fiocchi to Sister Maria Angela del Cielo, dated September 1765: "Love and go forward. Go forward and love. Love is the goal of the blessed and it ought to be the goal of the living as well. Place all your attention on love, dwell in love, clothe yourself in love, breath love, act for love, be insatiable for love, and may love be your all."

All: *The assembly sings the refrain of "Eye Has Not Seen" as a response.*

Reader 6: This is from a letter of Father Thomas Bridgett, C.Ss.R., to a sister and dated Easter Monday 1872: "It has always been my principle in direction to interfere as little as possible with my penitent's liberty; very seldom to suggest anything; never to oblige unless when I am sure that the law of God obliged; never to forbid unless I am sure that the love of God forbids; rarely to dissuade unless I saw that the conscience was already dissuading—in a word, simply to follow God's grace in my penitents, not to try to go before it or to take the place of it. My conviction has always been that the notion of direction is not that of impulsion. The Spirit of God must give the impulse, the human director only study it in the soul of the penitents and counsel them how to obey it, help them to remove obstacles, try to discern between the movements of nature and those of grace, and solve doubts to the best of his power."

All: *The assembly sings the refrain of "Eye Has Not Seen" as a response.*

Reader 7: This is from a letter of Saint John Neumann to a religious superior: "I beg you to introduce as soon as possible all the spiritual exercises prescribed by the rules of your Order, for I wish your house to be a model of religious observance. I am not solicitous about its temporalities, Divine Providence will see that you always have what is necessary, if the sisters faithfully observe their rule and by their mutual love and harmony attract his blessing upon themselves. I exceedingly dislike that religious houses should depend on the favor of creditors. Let us trust in God and Saint Joseph. In God's own good time things will come right. Be satisfied with what is necessary for the present day and confide the future to God. I know this exacts great self-denial but it is the surest way of acting."

All: *The assembly sings the refrain of "Eye Has Not Seen" as a response.*

Reader 8: This is from a letter of Francis X. Schnuttgen, C.Ss.R., to Sister M. Genevieve, I.H.M.: "I feel sorry that no notes are published of the last Mother Teresa; but please do not neglect to write out, as completely as possible, a biography of Reverend Mother Teresa and in it to tell the truth, and the whole truth; gather quietly all the information you can get from all available sources. Take note of little incidents and anecdotes that show the virtues and character of the late Mother. It is strange that color should cause religious to have a prejudice against a very deserving person. The Spouse in the Canticles is called "*nigra sed formosa*," black but beautiful. I fear that some of the white opponents of good Mother Teresa are in reality more black than the one They disown as their mother.

Faith-Sharing

Presider: After hearing these letters read, I now invite members of the group to share their responses (with a neighbor or with the whole assembly) to the following question: Having heard these letters, how would you describe the Redemptorist approach to spiritual direction?

Closing Ritual

Presider: *The presider explains that each participant will be given a card and an envelope to send to someone who would like to hear from him or her. The presider hands the card to each participant saying, "Share what God in mercy has done for you."*

REDEMPTORISTS AS SPIRITUAL DIRECTORS

FINDING GOD IN THE MAILBOX

Closing Song

Presider: The assembly closes with verse 3 of "Eye Has Not Seen."

CELEBRATING THE REDEMPTORIST PIONEERS IN AMERICA

Environment: Symbols of the C.Ss.R. presence in the United States are arranged in a prominent place: a map of the U.S.; an American flag; the C.Ss.R. mission cross; photographs of New York Harbor in the nineteenth century; six cards on each of which is written the name of one Redemptorist pioneer; six candles, one placed by each card. The candle is lighted as the story of each man is told.

Opening Song

"God of Our Fathers": *Worship #764*

Introductory Scripture

Presider: This is a reading from the Book of Sirach: 44:1–15.

Readings

Presider: On Wednesday, June 20, 1832, six Redemptorist missionaries stepped ashore from the brig Potomac onto American soil and the charism of Alphonsus, one hundred years old, reached a decisive moment of growth. We celebrate the memory of these men, our brothers: Simon Saenderl, Francis Tschenhens, Francis Haetscher, James Kohler, Aloysius Schuh, and Wenceslaus Witopil. They are the first in the long line of Redemptorists to preach the good news of plentiful redemption in the United States. They are the forefathers of our American Redemptorist family; we turn back the pages of our family album and listen to their stories. Like the people of Israel, we praise those godly men, our ancestors. In our gatherings their wisdom is retold and our assembly proclaims their praise.

Reader 1: I am Simon Saenderl, the superior of the mission, although my life in this strange new land was nothing like that of a Father Rector in Europe. I was already a priest when I entered the Congregation, and professed only three years. I was appointed by Father Passerat to lead the sons of Alphonsus to America. Perhaps I wasn't the best choice. From the beginning we were plagued by the conditions in the American frontier and misunderstood by the superiors in Europe. But for all that I did much good. The native peoples of the Midwest responded to my preaching—I wrote over four hundred pages of sermons and instructions in the Ottawa Indian language. Through a misunderstanding, I was expelled from the Congregation; I worked in Canada and made a pilgrimage to the Holy Land. I finally found peace as a Trappist monk in the Abbey of Gethsemani.

All: Let us praise these godly men, our ancestors, the abounding glory of the Most High's portion.

Reader 2: I am Francis Tschenhens. If you can't say my name just call me "Jennings" like the Irish immigrants did. Little did I dream as I stood in front of my Latin class in Fribourg that I would end up a pioneer, riding on horseback for hours throughout Ohio. (The future Rector Major Nicholas Mauron, by the way, was one of my pupils.) I fought to establish the first C.Ss.R. community in the village of Norwalk, but my superiors didn't agree. I spent the rest of my life in our foundations which mushroomed across the eastern U.S. In Pittsburgh, I was the novice master of John Neumann (my students turned out better than I did). I did succeed in establishing in Norwalk the first Church in the new world dedicated to our Father Saint Alphonsus.

All: These were godly men whose virtues have not been forgotten; their heritage remains with their descendants.

Reader 3: I am Francis Haetscher. I was what you might call a juvenile delinquent and ran away from home until I was converted by the preaching of Clement Hofbauer and reconciled with my mother. I was forty-eight when I was sent to America and seventeen years professed. I really should have been the superior! I preached the first mission on American soil at Saint Mary's in Toledo. I nursed victims of the cholera epidemic, befriended Father Gabriel Richard, apostle of the Church in Detroit, and fought Jansenism with the kind spirit of Saint Alphonsus. There were French priests in Michigan who actually taught that a passionate kiss even between married people is a mortal sin. In the end, it all tired me out and, in 1838 at age fifty-three, I asked permission to return to Europe to live out my Redemptorist life there.

All: For all time may their progeny endure and may their glory never be blotted out.

Reader 4: I am James Kohler. I was the youngest of the pioneer group, just twenty-seven, and professed a Redemptorist brother just three years. Almost on arrival, Father Tschenhens lent me to the diocesan seminary in Cincinnati as a cook. I didn't become a Redemptorist to cook for diocesans! Later I rejoined the community in Norwalk where an ex-nun friend of Tschenhens ordered me around as if she were superior. This is not what I had in mind when I entered religious life! I took off and sold oil on the streets of New York trying to earn money for my return passage to Europe. My confreres did try to get me to come back a number of times. I did return in 1840 and went as cook to Saint John's in Baltimore, but it was all too much for me and in 1847 I left for good. I ran a tavern near Saint Alphonsus Church and occasionally I'd buy the fathers a beer and talk about the old days.

All: Their bodies lie in peace but their name lives on and on.

Reader 5: I am Aloysius Schuh. They used to call me "Brother Cyclops" because like those mythological figures I was a skilled blacksmith and metalworker. I taught these skills to the native Americans in Michigan. In Norwalk, often when the priests were away, I would lead the people in prayer on Sunday, reading and explaining the readings of the day. For a while I went back to Europe in the hopes of a more regular religious life but the call of the American mission was too strong, and I returned in 1841 and spent the rest of my life in amazement of the growth of the American province.

All: At gatherings their wisdom is retold and the assembly proclaims their praise.

Reader 6: I am Wenceslaus Witopil. I was a little more than a year professed as a Redemptorist brother when I was sent to the American mission. It was far from being to my liking. I wanted community life not the wild life of a fur trading outpost or an Indian reservation. In 1835, I returned to Europe and spent the rest of my Redemptorist life telling tales at recreation that made everyone grateful they had not been sent to America.

Faith-Sharing

Presider: We have listened to the stories of the pioneers of the American mission. They were men much like ourselves. They were gifted and flawed. They had moments of great heroism and accomplishment. They had moments of weakness and failure. What unites us to them is that each of them, some for a lifetime and some for a few years, gave themselves to the following of Jesus the Redeemer on American soil. They are the forefathers of our family. After a few moments of silent reflection, share with some of your neighbors or with the whole group a story of a Redemptorist pioneer that you knew or that you are! Tell the story of the beginnings of something new—a new foundation, mission, or apostolate. What were the qualities of those men that moved them to express the charism of Alphonsus in a new way or new place?

Litany

The verses of the litany may be said by the presider or by different members of the assembly.

Presider: For the dream of Alphonsus who saw his Congregation spreading its wings to cover the earth…

All: We give thanks and praise.

Presider: For the vision of Clement who poured over maps of North America and for Joseph Passerat who put that vision into practice…

All: We give thanks and praise.

Presider: For the lives and ministries of our American forefathers: Simon, Francis, James, Aloysius, Francis, Wenceslaus…

All: We give thanks and praise.

Presider: For all the Redemptorists who have worked since 1832 in the American provinces and their missions…

All: We give thanks and praise.

Presider: That we might be faithful to our tradition of risk-taking and innovation…

All: Holy Redeemer, hear our prayer.

Presider: For forgiveness for our fears and our inertia…

All: Holy Redeemer, hear our prayer.

Presider: That many will follow after us in the Redemptorist vocation…

All: Holy Redeemer, hear our prayer.

Presider: That we will continue to work to bring American culture and the Gospel into fruitful dialogue…

All: Holy Redeemer, hear our prayer.

Presider: We now invite assembly members to add spontaneous petitions to these intercessions.

Closing Antiphon

Presider: We conclude our prayer in song to the Immaculate Virgin Mary. May her *Magnificat* become true in our land—that the lowly be raised to high places, the hungry be filled, and may every soul proclaim the greatness of God. Now let us sing *"Salve Regina."* The words to this antiphon may be found on page 57.

26

FULL AND EQUAL PARTNERS: CELEBRATING REDEMPTORIST/LAY COLLABORATION

Environment: A display consisting of a bowl of water and the paschal candle or other large candle—symbols of our common baptism—is arranged.

Opening Song

"The Church's One Foundation": *Gather Comprehensive* #661
"City of God": *Gather Comprehensive* #678:
"Gather Us In": *Gather Comprehensive* #744:

Call to Prayer

Presider: Redemptorist life has never been possible without the support and encouragement of the laity. As we Redemptorists have touched and changed the life of the Church, so we have been touched and changed by the people with whom and for whom we have been called to minister. As we look to the third century of our Congregation's life, we are exploring new ways of joining with laywomen and laymen in the mission to bring the good news of plentiful redemption to those most in need of God's mercy. We celebrate the ways in which Redemptorists and the laity have collaborated in the past, and we pray that the Spirit of God guide our steps into a new future together. Let us pray:

All: Spirit of Jesus the Redeemer, open us to your call.
You raise up hundreds of voices to proclaim your praise
and thousands of hands to build your reign on earth.
Make all the members of your Church more deeply conscious
of our baptismal commitment to renew the world in your image.
May all Redemptorists follow the example of Alphonsus
who wished to form communities of prayer and mission for all your people.

Readings and Responses

Reader 1: This is a reading from the First Letter to the Corinthians: 12:12–13; 27–31.

All: *The assembly sings the refrain from "The Spirit of God" (Gather Comprehensive #458):*

> The Spirit of God rests upon me.
> The Spirit of God consecrates me.
> The Spirit of God bids me go forth
> to proclaim his peace, his joy.

Reader 2: We remember the lay leaders of the evening chapels in Naples whom Alphonsus empowered to be leaders of spiritual development: Pietro Barbarese, Luca Nardone, Bernardino the cowherd, Leonardo who sold chestnuts on the streets; we recall as well the laywomen trained by Alphonsus whose names history has not recorded.

All: *The assembly sings the refrain from "The Spirit of God" (Gather Comprehensive #458).*

Reader 3: We remember the circles of laity that gathered around Clement: rich and poor, young and old, students and soldiers; professors and merchants; together discovering ways to preach the Gospel anew in a world of radical change.

All: *The assembly sings the refrain from "The Spirit of God" (Gather Comprehensive #458).*

Reader 4: We remember Captain Henri Belletable, an engineering officer who knew the misery of the poor workers in the factories of nineteenth-century Belgium. Together with the tailor Charles Hacken and under the direction of Redemptorist Victor Deschamps, he founded the Confraternity of the Holy Family—groups of prayer and social support for those who were ashamed to go to church in their worker's clothes.

All: *The assembly sings the refrain from "The Spirit of God" (Gather Comprehensive #458).*

Reader 5: We remember Concha Espina, Spanish poet and novelist, who died in Madrid in 1955. She was a friend of the Redemptorists and celebrated them in her newspaper column; "in all parts of the world they are friends of the people."

All: *The assembly sings the refrain from "The Spirit of God" (Gather Comprehensive #458).*

Reader 6: We remember all those countless benefactors who have supported the Redemptorist mission. From the people, rich and poor, who worked alongside Alphonsus to build the house in Ciorani to those who even today support the Redemptorist mission with their interest, financial aid, and prayers. We remember those countless people who are our friends and coworkers: religious education teachers, liturgical musicians and ministers, schoolteachers, bingo workers and cooks at parish functions. May God bless the generosity of those who have received us into their homes and their hearts.

All: *The assembly sings the refrain from "The Spirit of God"* (Gather Comprehensive #458).

Reader 7: We look with hope to those new forms of Redemptorist and lay collaboration called for by the Twenty-First General Chapter, especially the Lay Missionaries of the Most Holy Redeemer. We rejoice that "the Holy Spirit today is urging lay people to a greater collaboration in the evangelizing of the poor," and we believe that "this constitutes a precious sign of the times for the ecclesial and Redemptorist community" (Communicanda #4, *Collaboration Between the Redemptorist Community and the Laity,* n.10).

All: *The assembly sings the refrain from "The Spirit of God"* (Gather Comprehensive #458).

Faith-Sharing

Presider: I invite you now to share with the whole group or with a few of your neighbors an experience of collaboration between Redemptorists and the laity. What does the Redemptorist charism have to offer to such a collaboration? What can the Redemptorists learn from such a collaboration?

Ritual

Presider: By Baptism we have all been called to follow Jesus the Redeemer. We have all been anointed with the Spirit to preach the Good News to the poor, to liberate the oppressed, and to proclaim a time of God's favor. Together we extend our hands to bless this water which we will use to recall our baptism.

All extend their hands while the presider or another prays:

Life-giving Spirit of God, move upon this water. Move upon your people gathered here to celebrate your wondrous gifts bestowed in abundance on your church. May this water remind us of the Bay of Naples where our charism was born and where Alphonsus taught God's love to the poor and learned it from them. May this water remind us of the tears of those who suffer injustice and of the sweat of those who labor to overcome it. Revive in us the grace of our common baptism and strengthen us for our common mission—to renew creation in the image of Jesus the Redeemer. We pray in his name, Jesus, Redeemer and friend.

All: *The assembly sings the refrain from "The Spirit of God":* (Gather Comprehensive #458).

The assembly approaches the bowl of water in twos, each making the sign of the cross on the other's forehead.

Presider: This reading is from an address by Juan Manuel Lasso de la Vega y Miranda, C.Ss.R., Superior General Emeritus: "The disciples gathered in the upper room to pray for the outpouring of the Holy Spirit together with Mary the Mother of Jesus. As followers of Alphonsus, we have always found Mary at the heart of our life and ministry. May Mary's presence and prayers guide our efforts towards a Spirit-filled future of collaboration of Redemptorists and laity as full and equal partners." Let us now pray:

Presider: Mother of the Red%emer…

All: Hail full of grace.

Presider: Woman filled with the Spirit…

All: Hail full of grace.

Presider: Lay missionary of Plentiful Redemption…

All: Hail full of grace.

Presider: Companion and Teacher of the Apostles…

All: Hail full of grace.

Closing Antiphon

Presider: We close this prayer service by singing the "*Salve Regina.*" The words to this antiphon may be found on page 57. (*Note: Alternately, one of the opening songs may be used in closing.*)

HEAR THE VOICE OF ANNA: THE FEMININE AND THE REDEMPTORIST CHARISM

Environment: On display is an image of Our Lady of Perpetual Help and pictures of the women mentioned in the prayer service or other current or past women collaborators with the Redemptorists; enough small stones to give one to each member of the group.

Opening Song

"For All the Saints": *Gather Comprehensive #793*
"Ye Watchers and Ye Holy Ones": *Gather Comprehensive #794*

Readings and Responses

Reader 1: This is a reading from the Gospel of Luke: 2:25–38.

Presider: Each night for centuries, the Church has prayed the Canticle of Simeon, the righteous elder who rejoiced to see redemption's dawning. Another was in the Temple that day—Anna the prophet. Her words were not recorded; her song remains unsung. Too often the voice of women's experience have gone unheard in the Church. Too often the presence of the feminine in our charism and history has gone uncelebrated. Let us listen today in prayer for the song of Anna, the voice of women in our life, history, and ministry.

Pause for Silent Prayer

Reader 2: Hear the voice of Mary, who, in the grotto of Scala, told the young Alphonsus many beautiful things about the future of our Congregation that consoled and sustained him all his life.

Pause for Silent Prayer

Reader 3: Hear the gentle voice of Anna Cavalieri, the mother of Saint Alphonsus. She taught the Doctor of Prayer how to pray and all his life he used a little handwritten book of prayers that she gave him.

Pause for Silent Prayer

Reader 4: Hear the courageous voice of Maria Celeste Crostarosa who was faithful to her vision to be a *viva memoria* of the Redeemer despite misunderstanding and scorn.

Pause for Silent Prayer

Reader 5: Hear the voice of the women of the Evening Chapels, who prayed with Alphonsus and who sang his songs as lullabies to their children.

Pause for Silent Prayer

Reader 6: Hear the voices of Saint Brianna Cafara, Sister Giovanna della Croce, of the scrupulous laywoman Maria, who found in Alphonsus an understanding heart and a discerning spiritual director.

Pause for Silent Prayer

Reader 7: Hear the voices of Eugénie Dijon (Mother Marie-Alphonse) and Antonia Welsersheimb (Sister Marie-Anne Joseph) who were so captivated by the spirit of Alphonsus that they left their homes in Germany to enter the Redemptoristines in Saint Agatha of the Goths. They founded the Redemptoristines in Vienna from where they spread throughout the world.

Pause for Silent Prayer

Reader 8: Hear the voice of Mother Teresa Maxis, foundress of the Sisters, Servants of the Immaculate Heart of Mary. Because of clericalism and racism, she was exiled from her community for fourteen years. Her faithful Redemptorist friend, Egidius Smulders wrote of her, "She loved Saint Alphonsus too much; therefore she suffers exile."

Pause for Silent Prayer

Reader 9: Hear the voice of Mother Mary Elizabeth Lange, foundress of the Oblate Sisters of Providence, the first religious community for women of color. When the Oblates were in danger of suppression, the Redemptorist Father Thaddeus Anwander appealed for their survival to the Archbishop of Baltimore and pleaded, on his knees for their survival.

Pause for Silent Prayer

Reader 10: Hear the voices of Mother Theresa Gerhardingder and Mother Caroline Friess of the School Sisters of Notre Dame. With Saint John Neumann they traveled from New York to Milwaukee to make provision for the education of immigrant children in nineteenth-century America.

Pause for Silent Prayer

Reader 11: Hear the voice of Mother Mercedes de Molina, who evangelized the jungles of Ecuador in the nineteenth century. She died holding the image of Our Mother of Perpetual Help, with her Redemptorist confessor and friend Father Peter Clam at her side.

Pause for Silent Prayer

Reader 12: Hear the voice of Blessed Elizabeth of the Trinity, who found the courage to follow her vocation to the Carmelites on a Redemptorist mission. She wrote, "How beautifully the Redemptorists speak of the love of God!"

Pause for Silent Prayer

Reader 13: Hear the voices of the countless women whose names are unremembered but who shared throughout history in the spirit of Alphonsus to preach the redeeming love of the Redeemer to the most abandoned.

Pause for Silent Prayer

Faith-Sharing

Presider: Share with the members of the group or with one or two neighbors a story of a woman, past or present, who seems to you to have been a particular example of the spirit of Saint Alphonsus.

Ritual

Presider: Let us stand and listen to the account of the first witnesses to the Resurrection, the holy women who overcame their fear and proclaimed the Gospel of the One Risen from the dead.

Reader 14: This is a reading from the Gospel of Mark: 16:1–8.

Presider: The holy women did not let the obstacle of the stone at the mouth of the tomb prevent them from setting out to anoint the body of Jesus. They acted despite their fears and their courage was rewarded beyond their powers to imagine. They also overcame their fear of speaking and so through their testimony we received the message of the Gospel.

I invite you to come forward and to take one of these small stones. Put it in a place where you can see it often. Let it remind you of the courage of these women who overcame fears and obstacles in the service of the Gospel. They gave voice to the silent song of Anna and the world rings with the good news of death vanquished and Life triumphant. Let it strengthen you to overcome your own fears and obstacles in the following of Jesus.

Blessing

Members of the assembly come forward and take a stone. After all have taken ! stone the prayer service is concluded with the following blessing.

Presider: May the God who shakes heaven and earth,
whom death could not contain,
who lives to disturb and heal us,
bless you with power to go forth
and proclaim the Gospel.
All: Amen.

Closing Antiphon

Presider: Let us now sing together the antiphon "*Salve Regina.*" The words may be found on page 57.

HEAR THE VOICE OF ANNA
CSSR
THE FEMININE AND THE REDEMPTORIST CHARISM

EAT THE BOOK!
THE CONSTITUTIONS AS A SOURCE
OF REDEMPTORIST SPIRITUALITY

Environment: On display is a copy of the Constitutions surrounded by flowers and candles; a plate with pieces of candy (for example, chocolate kisses) and/or sweet fruit (for example, grapes).

Opening Song

Presider: Let us open this prayer service by singing the following verses to the tune of "*Laast Uns Erfruen*," that is, "Ye Watchers and Ye Holy Ones," *Gather Comprehensive* #794.

1. In Al-phon-sus we claim to be,
   Through all the world one fam-i-ly,
   O -, Praise God, Cop-i-o-sa
   A liv-ing her-i-tage we share,
   of mis-sion, com-mon life and pray'r.
   Cop-i-o-sa! Al-le-lu-ia! Co-pi-o-sa, Al-le-lu-ia! Co-pi-o-sa!

2. To East and West, to South and North;
   Pro-phets of mer-cy now go forth.
   Tell the good news
   Cop-i-o-sa.
   Through-out the u-ni-verse re-lease,
   God's reign of jus-tice, love, and peace!
   Cop-i-o-sa! Al-le-lu-ia! Co-pi-o-sa, Al-le-lu-ia! Co-pi-o-sa!

3. How beau-ti-ful up-on the earth,
   the feet of those who bring God's word,
   Preach the Gos-pel, Co-pi-o-sa!
   All through the world our voice re-sounds,
   Plen-ti-ful re-demp-tion a-bounds.
   Cop-i-o-sa! Al-le-lu-ia! Co-pi-o-sa, Al-le-lu-ia! Co-pi-o-sa!

Scripture Reading

Reader 1: This is a reading from the Book of Ezekiel: 3:1–15.

Presider: Dominic Blassuci, one of the holy men of the first generation of the Congregation, had written on his copy of the Rule the text from the prophet Ezekiel *Commede librum! Eat the Book!* He knew that the Redemptorist Rule had to take flesh in him. It had to become bone and sinew for him. It had to be transformed from a cold text into fiery energy for mission. It had to energize him to go to peo0le in the exile of alienation and to proclaim the Gospel of welcome and return. We gather together to chew over our Constitutions in prayer, to be nourished on this book and to find the energy to preach the Good News to the boundaries of our millennium.

Reading of the Constitutions

A portion of the Constitutions is now read. If the group wishes, before the reading of the Constitutions, the book may be venerated with incense while an Alleluia is sung. Since the Constitutions represent for us the particular way in which the gospel is lived in the Redemptorist Congregation, it might be appropriate to venerate them in the same way we venerate the gospel book. After the readings, the book of the Constitutions may be passed through the group and venerated with a kiss, a traditional practice in the Congregation.

The group may choose to read a portion from each chapter of the Constitutions, for example, Chapter 1, Paragraph 6; Chapter 2, Paragraph 21; Chapter 3, Paragraphs 52 and 53; Chapter 4, Paragraph 78. The group might also choose to read one entire chapter of the Constitutions— each one reading after the other in turns until an entire chapter has been read.

Faith-Sharing

Presider: Now let us share with the group or each other our responses to the following questions:

What am I called to do upon hearing these words of the Constitutions? What are we called to do upon hearing these words of the Constitutions?

Intercessions

Presider: Let us pray for the grace to enflesh the values of our Constitutions in our lives and our communities. *(Note: The citations of the Constitutions given in the petitions are only for reference and should not be read as part of the petition.)*

All: Holy Redeemer, fill us with your life.

Presider: *(From the Historical Preface):* That we, like Saint Alphonsus, may "never be shaken in the belief that [our] Congregation, under the protection of the Most Blessed Virgin Mary, would labor vigorously together with the Church in the task of winning the world for Christ," we pray...

All: Holy Redeemer, fill us with your life.

Presider: *(From Chapter 1, Paragraph 9):* That we might give witness to the "charity of Christ and do all in [our] power to make ourselves neighbors to everybody," we pray...

All: Holy Redeemer, fill us with your life.

Presider: *(From Chapter 2, Paragraph 22):* That we might join our "prayers and deliberations, [our] labors and sufferings, [our] successes and failures and [our] material goods as well, for the service of the gospel," we pray...

All: Holy Redeemer, fill us with your life.

Presider: *(From Chapter 3, Paragraph 51):* That we may become "signs and witness before people of the power of Jesus' resurrection, proclaiming new and eternal life," we pray...

All: Holy Redeemer, fill us with your life.

Presider: *(From Chapter 4, Paragraph 78):* That we might "learn progressively what the following of Christ demands...and thus become true missionaries," we pray...

All: Holy Redeemer, fill us with your life.

Presider: *(From Chapter 5, Paragraph 92):* That we may grow in the knowledge that to each one of us is "given the manifestation of the Spirit for the sake of the common good," we pray...

All: Holy Redeemer, fill us with your life.

Presider: I now invite members of the assembly to add their own spontaneous petitions to these intercessions.

Ritual

Presider: In the Jewish tradition, when parents first teach their children the words of the Scripture they give them a taste of honey for each word or verse learned so that they might know the sweetness of the study of the Word of God. Our Constitutions are a sacred text for us and the most important source of Redemptorist spirituality. I invite you now to eat something sweet that you may know the sweetness of the study of the spirit of Saint Alphonsus.

The presider passes the plate with the candy/fruit through the assembly.

Presider: I invite you know to renew our religious profession; our commitment to make the vision of our Constitutions a reality.

All: Following Christ, the Savior of the world,
with fidelity and perseverance,
I *(each confrere says his name one after the other in turn after which*
all continue together):
renew my vows of chastity, poverty, and of obedience,
together with my vow and oath of perseverance,
according to the spirit and way of life
proper to the Congregation of the Most Holy Redeemer,
so that apostolic zeal may increase in me and
in the whole Congregation,
for the good of the whole Church. Amen.

Closing Antiphon

Presider: Let us now close by singing the "*Salve Regina.*" The words to this antiphon may be found on page 57.

EAT THE BOOK

THE CONSTITUTIONS AS A SOURCE OF REDEMPTORIST SPIRITUALITY

CSSR

A NOVENA OF MADONNAS: ALPHONSIAN DEVOTION TO THE BLESSED VIRGIN MARY

Environment: A display is arranged with the following: an image or picture of Our Lady of Perpetual Help or of one of Alphonsus's paintings of Mary; an empty vase into which each reader will place a flower after each reading.

Introduction

Presider: May the grace and peace of Jesus, Son of Mary, be with you.
All: And also with you.

Call to Prayer

Presider: Throughout his life, through preaching and prayer, through music, art, and poetry, Alphonsus Liguori sought to proclaim the "glories of Mary." All of his many works were written under the gaze of Our Lady of Good Counsel. Confidence in her intercession gave him courage to undertake great risks like the founding of the Redemptorist Congregation. He found that sermons on her could turn the heart of the hardest sinner to conversion. Let now try to imagine Alphonsus at his harpsichord composing his song, *"O Bella Mia Speranza."* May we, like Alphonsus, find in Mary a reflection of God's beauty and a channel of God's hope.

Meditation Song

"O Bella Mia Speranza" *is played while the assembly pauses for silent meditation.*

Readings and Responses

Each reader has a flower which he or she will place before the image of Mary after the reading.

Presider: The novena was a form of prayer that was very meaningful to Alphonsus. He wanted the Redemptorists to prepare for each of the principal feasts of Our Lady by a novena of prayer. We reflect today on nine images or tit,es of Mary that spoke to Alphonsus and which form the tradition of Marian devotion that he left to his Congregation as a precious heritage.

Reader 1: Alphonsus, on the day of your conversion, you left you cavalier's sword at the feet of Mary, Our Lady of Mercy, Ransomer of Captives. May we also find in Mary a model of the freedom of the sons and daughters of God.

All: *The assembly sings the refrain of the Lourdes hymn: Ave, Ave, Ave, Maria; Ave, Ave, Ave, Maria.*

Reader 2: Alphonsus, in the abandoned chapel of Scala, you venerated the image of Mary, Mother of the Redeemer. In one arm she held the open Bible, the Word of God; in the other, the child Jesus, the Word Made Flesh. By our preaching of God's word, may God again take flesh in the hearts of believers.

All: *The assembly sings the refrain of the Lourdes hymn: Ave, Ave, Ave, Maria; Ave, Ave, Ave, Maria.*

Reader 3: Alphonsus, on the missions you displayed a painting of Mary the Shepherdess. You wanted the peasants and goatherds to experience the Redeemer and his mother as ones like themselves, sharing their lives and knowing their struggles. May our ministries keep us close to God's people and may we ever proclaim the God who is Emmanuel, the God who is with us.

All: *The assembly sings the refrain of the Lourdes hymn: Ave, Ave, Ave, Maria; Ave, Ave, Ave, Maria.*

Reader 4: Alphonsus, you painted an image of the Madonna of the Holy Spirit. You show Mary lifting her cloak to reveal the dove of the Holy Spirit in her heart. May we be ever mindful that we are the dwelling places of God; give us a deep respect for conscience, the holy temple in which God speaks.

All: *The assembly sings the refrain of the Lourdes hymn: Ave, Ave, Ave, Maria; Ave, Ave, Ave, Maria.*

Reader 5: Alphonsus gave Mary, the Immaculate Conception, as the patroness of our Congregation. Mary Immaculate is the great sign of God's original dream for creation. May Mary Immaculate draw us to hunger and thirst for intimacy with God.

All: *The assembly sings the refrain of the Lourdes hymn: Ave, Ave, Ave, Maria; Ave, Ave, Ave, Maria.*

Reader 6: Alphonsus, you wrote your many works under the gaze of the image of Our Lady of Good Counsel. May we experience Mary as the woman of sage advice, as the spiritual director without equal.

All: *The assembly sings the refrain of the Lourdes hymn: Ave, Ave, Ave, Maria; Ave, Ave, Ave, Maria.*

Reader 7: Alphonsus, you saw Mary, Our Lady of Sorrows, as the midwife of the Church, born from the open heart of Jesus on Calvary. May we imitate her courage and have the strength to be companions of your suffering people.

All: *The assembly sings the refrain of the Lourdes hymn: Ave, Ave, Ave, Maria; Ave, Ave, Ave, Maria.*

Reader 8: Alphonsus, you wrote that, after the ascension of Jesus, Mary remained on earth to attend to the preaching of the Gospel. For you Mary was the Missionary. Make us ever conscious of Mary, present and active, among God's people today.

All: *The assembly sings the refrain of the Lourdes hymn: Ave, Ave, Ave, Maria; Ave, Ave, Ave, Maria.*

Reader 9: Alphonsus, you probably never saw the image so dear to your brothers, Our Mother of Perpetual Help. Yet you were moved by the conviction that Mary was tireless is coming to the aid of God's people. May our devotion to Our Mother of Perpetual Help energize us to come to the aid of those most in need of God's mercy. May we know the truth of your words, "Works of mercy are the things which please the Mother of Mercy most."

Faith-Sharing

Presider: I now invite members of the assembly to share their responses to this question: Which of these Alphonsian titles of Mary speaks to you most at this moment and why?

Intercessions

Presider: Let us arrange ourselves into two choirs and pray to Mary in the words of Saint Alphonsus:

Choir 1: O Mary, Queen of Light…
Choir 2: Enlighten sinners and bring them to the heart of Jesus.
Choir 1: O Lady, by the love you bear to Jesus…
Choir 2: Help me to love him.
Choir 1: Hail, Daughter of God the Father.
Choir 2: Hail, Mother of God the Son.
Choir 1: Hail, Spouse of the Holy Spirit.
Choi2 2: Hail, Temple of the Trinity.

Presider: Alphonsus compared Mary to Ruth in the Old Testament. Just as Ruth went through the fields to pick the grain left by the gleaners, so Mary goes through the world and is God's instrument of grace for those who are not reached by the ordinary ministry of the Church. Let us now commend to the mercy of God those people and situations that are most in need of it.

Members of the assembly simply mention people, groups, or situations of need or alienated from God that they wish to commend to their prayers.

Closing Antiphon

Presider: Saint Alphonsus loved the "*Salve Regina*" above all other prayers to Mary. His *Glories of Mary* is nothing more than an extended commentary on that hymn. He told us to pray the "*Salve Regina*" each day to ask for the grace of perseverance in the way of discipleship. In union with the whole Church, with our father Alphonsus and with our Redemptorist confreres throughout history we honor the Mother of God in song:

All: *The assembly joins together in singing the "Salve Regina." The words to this antiphon may be found on page 57.*

A NOVENA OF MADONNAS:
Alphonsian Devotion to the BVM

30

ALPHONSUS AND CREATION

Environment: If it is possible, this prayer service should be held outdoors. If it must be held inside, the room should be decorated with as many elements of nature as possible: plants, rocks, a bowl of earth, flowers, animals (for example, goldfish, or birds). There is also a basket holding cards on which are written a number of practical suggestions for a more ecologically sound lifestyle. Some suggestions are given in the box at the end of this prayer service.

Opening Song

"For the Beauty of the Earth": *Gather Comprehensive #572*

Call to Prayer

Presider: Redemptorists, like all the citizens of our planet at the dawn of the third millennium, are becoming more conscious of the beauty and fragility of our environment and of our obligation to cherish and protect it. Among the "most abandoned" to whom we are especially called, we can number our planet itself which daily suffers the ravages of exploitatio.. We are conscious that the poor often suffer first and most seriously the effects of the devastation of our planet. As we seek to become better stewards of the creation God entrusted to our care, we can find much inspiration in the life and spirit of our father Alphonsus.

Readings and Responses

Reader 1: This is a reading from two works of Saint Alphonsus: *The Truth of the Faith* and a *Brief Dissertation Against the Errors of Modern Unbelievers*: "In the heavens above we observe the stars with their orderly movements. We see the sun in swift movement whose rotation divides the day from night and the seasons one from another. We see the moon which speeds along as well, though less rapidly. It illumines the night for travelers and helps many things by its beneficial influence. We see the earth dressed in trees and grasses and which produces in due time fruits, grains, plants, metals, and so many other necessary and useful things for human life. The earth is made up of plains, of mountains, of forests, of rivers and fountains, all of which serve to form a home for humanity....Human beings, animals, plants, the skies, the planets, the seas and everything that we can see all demonstrate clearly the existence of the God who has created them all, as the Scriptures testify: 'For from the greatness and beauty of created things their original author, by analogy, is seen' (Wis 13:5); 'But now ask the beasts to teach you and the birds of the air to tell you. Which of these does not know that the hand of God has done this?' (Job 12:7.9); 'Ever since the creation of the world, the invisible attributes of eternal power and divinity have been able to be understood and perceived in created things'" (Rom 1:20).

All: *The assembly responds with the words of this psalm:*
The heavens are telling the glory of God;
the skies point to the art of their maker.
Day after day tells the story;
night after night recounts the tale.
No word, no sound, no voice is heard;
Yet the news goes out to all the earth;
to the ends of the world the message.
God has pitched a tent for the sun.
It comes forth like a bridegroom coming from his chamber,
like an athlete it joyfully runs its course.
From one end of the heavens to the other it runs;
nothing escapes its heat.
Glory to you, Source of all being, Eternal Word, and Holy Spirit.
As it was in the beginning, is now and will be forever. Amen.

Reader 2: The Jansenist theologians with whom Alphonsus battles saw created things as competitors with God for our love. Alphonsus instead saw all of creation as a mirror of the divine beauty and as so many gifts lavished on us by God to enkindle our love.

All: The heavens are telling the glory of God and all creation is singing for joy.

Reader 3: Alphonsus loved the countryside and made sure that all our first houses had gardens and orchards. He was a friend of farmers and knew the importance of cultivating the earth. He writes in a letter of Giovanni Mazzini about the new foundation in Deliceto: "There is a large vineyard that belongs to the house, a large well irrigated garden, and fountains with good clean water for drinking. There are already many fruit trees and I plan to plant many more."

All: Flowers and plants, bless the Lord. Praise and exalt God forever.

Reader 4: In 1761, Alphonsus, walking through the garden of Pagani, saw a baby sparrow trembling from cold. He picked it up carefully, carried it to the kitchen and warmed it by the fire. He cared for it until it was well enough to fly and then set it free.

All: Birds of the air, bless the Lord. Praise and exalt God forever.

Reader 5: Alphonsus drew a sphere showing the motion of the Earth and the planets for our students to study cosmology. His writings are filled with images of the natural world: the sun, moon, and stars; plants and animals; light and sound and color. In his work on the Incarnation, Alphonsus wrote, "At the birth of Jesus joy awoke and roamed creation free."

All: The heavens are telling the glory of God and all creation is singing for joy.

Faith-Sharing

Presider: I now invite members of the assembly to share with each other or with the group an encounter with the beauty of nature that gave you a sense of greater awe and reverence for God the Creator.

Ritual

Presider: The prayer of humanity give voice to the longing of all creation for completion. Let us embrace all the created world as we pray today.

The presider invites the assembly to stand and to face the north.

Reader 6: We pray for the grace of the North, the grace to believe that life continues hidden under the frozen earth; the grace to wait in persevering hope for the coming of spring; the grace to use the times of darkness for becoming quieter and going deeper.

All: We pray for the grace of the North, the grace of Alphonsus who met God in the dark night, who persevered in the face of failure, who brought love to cold hearts.

The presider invites the assembly to face the east.

Reader 7: We pray for the grace of the East, the place of the rising sun, the grace to believe in new beginnings, the grace not to be threatened by what is different, the grace to look hopefully for the dawn.

All: We pray for the grace of the East, the grace of Alphonsus the founder who brought to birth something new in the Church despite opposition.

The presider invites the assembly to face the south.